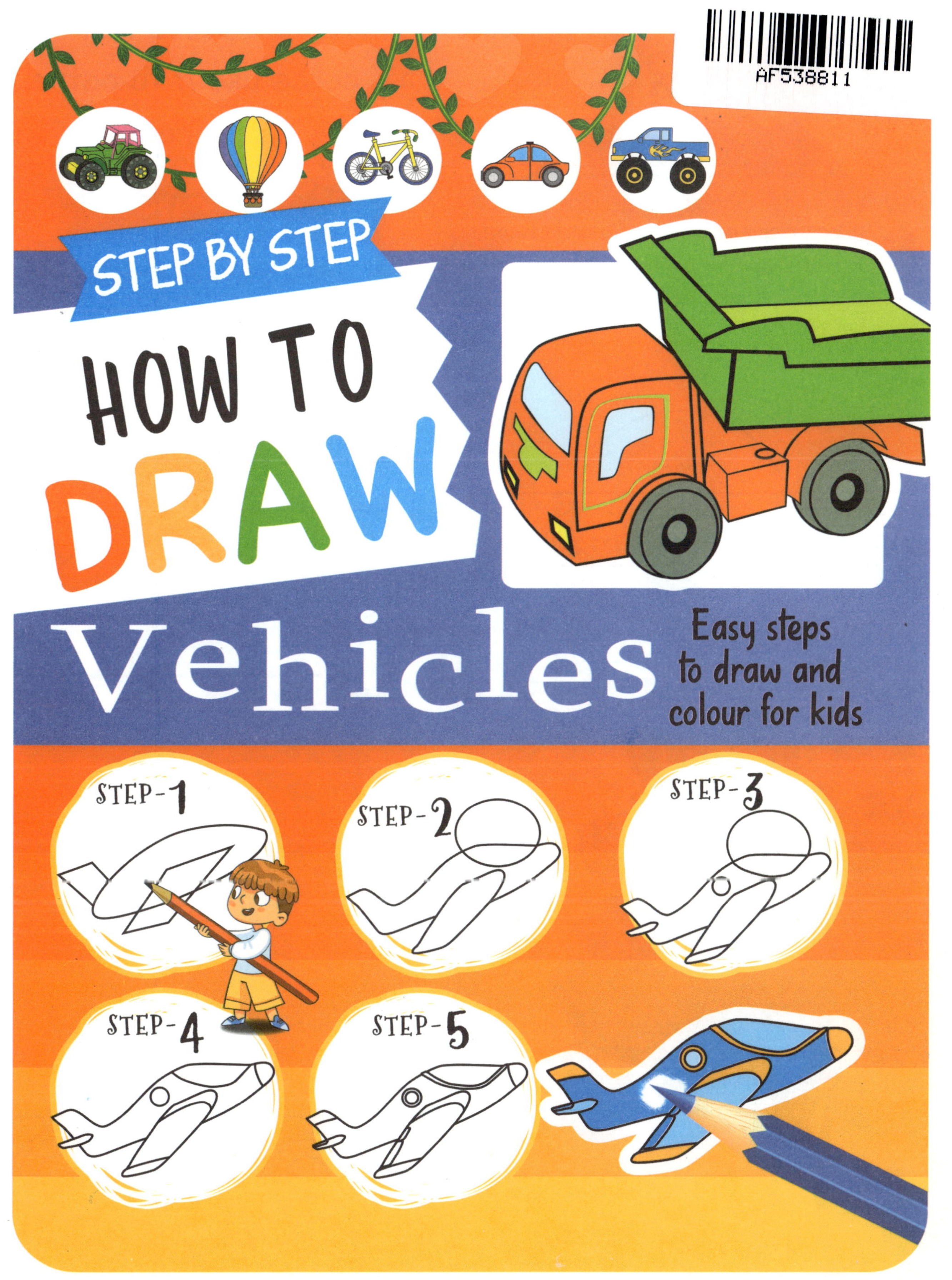
AF538811
STEP BY STEP
HOW TO
DRAW
Vehicles
Easy steps
to draw and
colour for kids
STEP-1
STEP-2
STEP-3
STEP-4
STEP-5

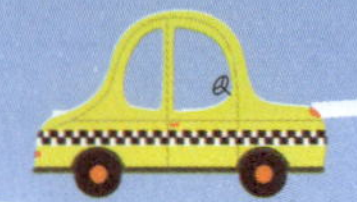

POLICE CAR

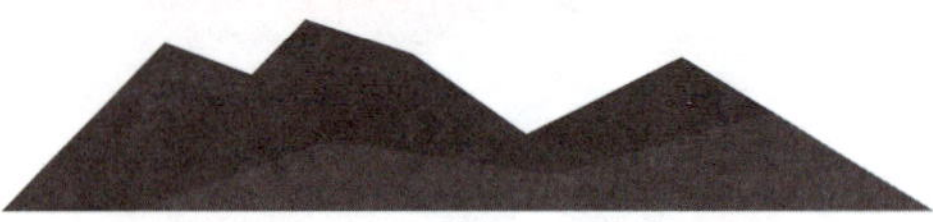

This is a police car. The police use it to patrol the streets.

1 Draw a rectangle with a big circle over it. Draw a small circle on the left. Draw another circle at the back, intersecting the big circle.

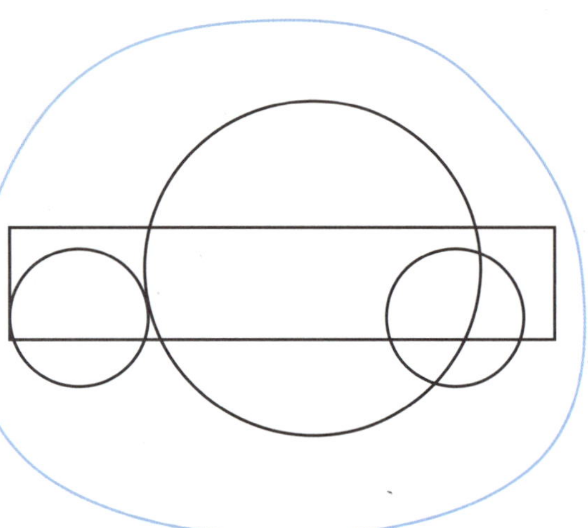

2 Draw a line from the middle of the rectang cutting across the big circle. Draw a bar for light and the bumper. Erase unwanted line

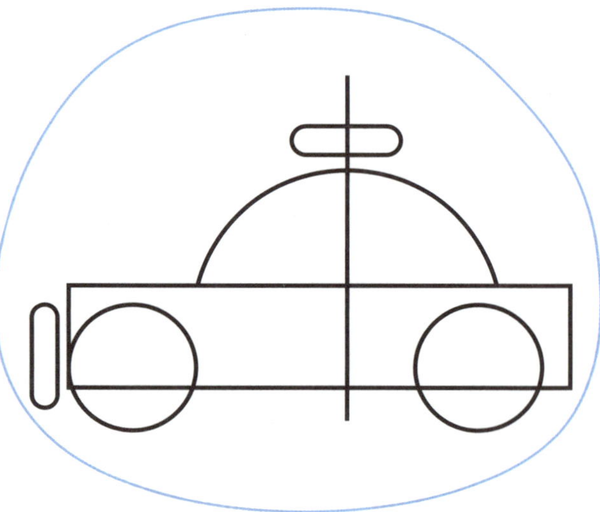

3 Draw circles for wheels. Draw a side mirror. Erase unwanted lines.

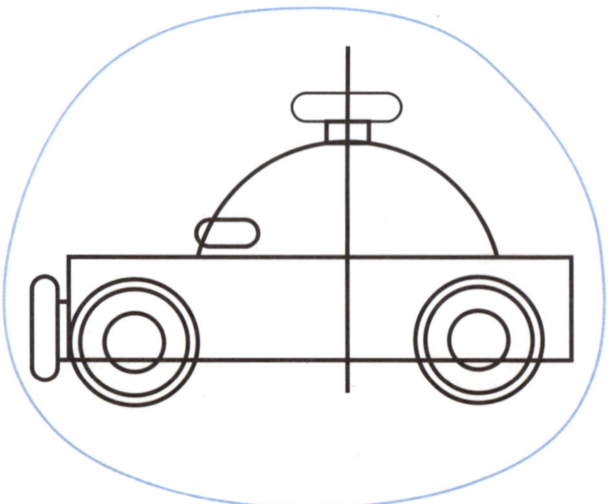

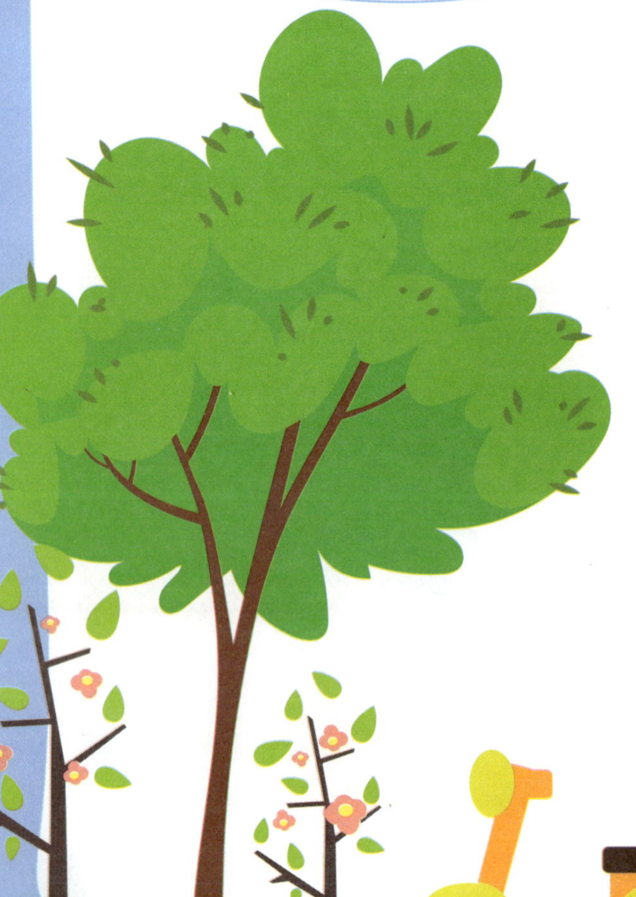

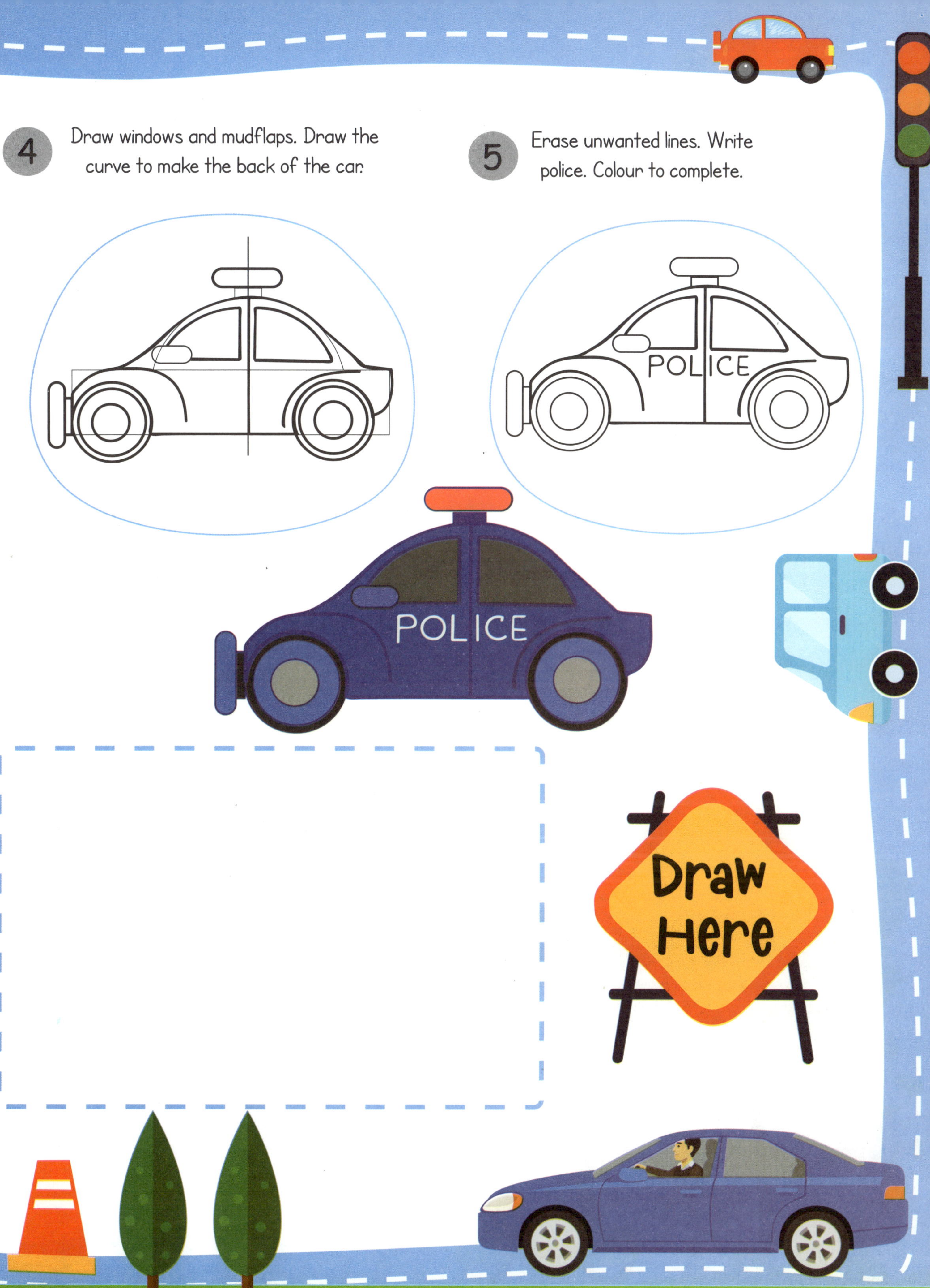
4
Draw windows and mudflaps. Draw the curve to make the back of the car.
5
Erase unwanted lines. Write police. Colour to complete.
POLICE
POLICE
Draw Here

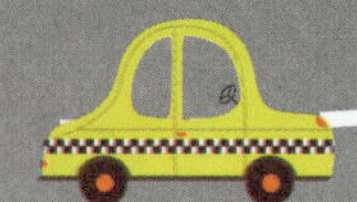

BICYCLE

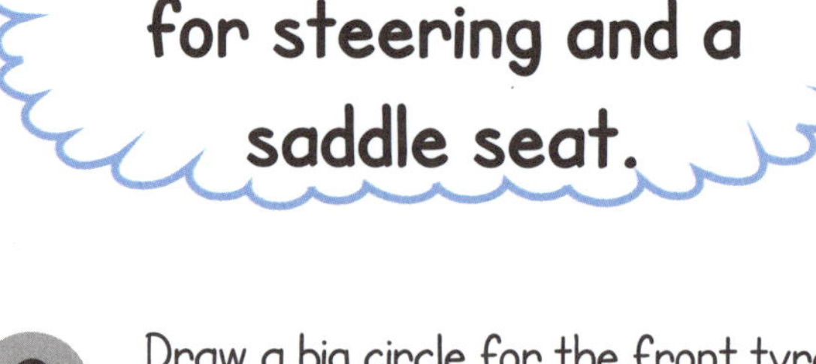

1 Draw a big circle with a small circle joining it on the right. Draw lines from the small circle.

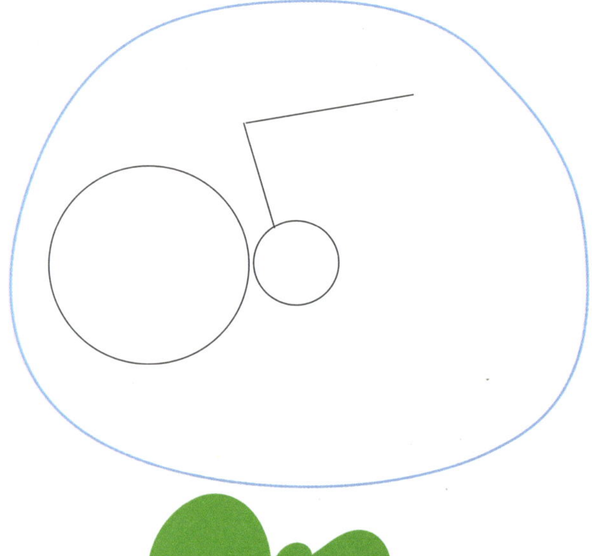

2 Draw a big circle for the front tyre. Draw lines for a chain and bars. Draw circles for spokes.

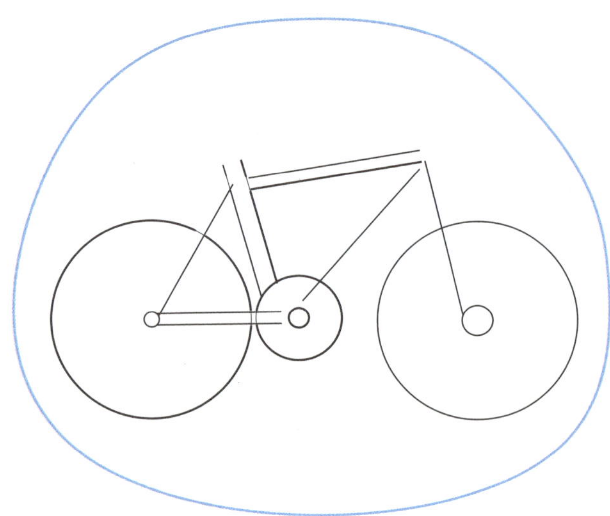

3 Draw lines to make the handle and the body. Draw a curve for the seat.

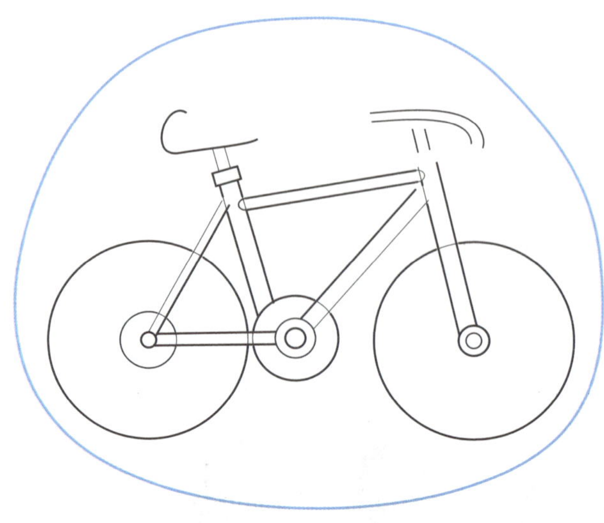

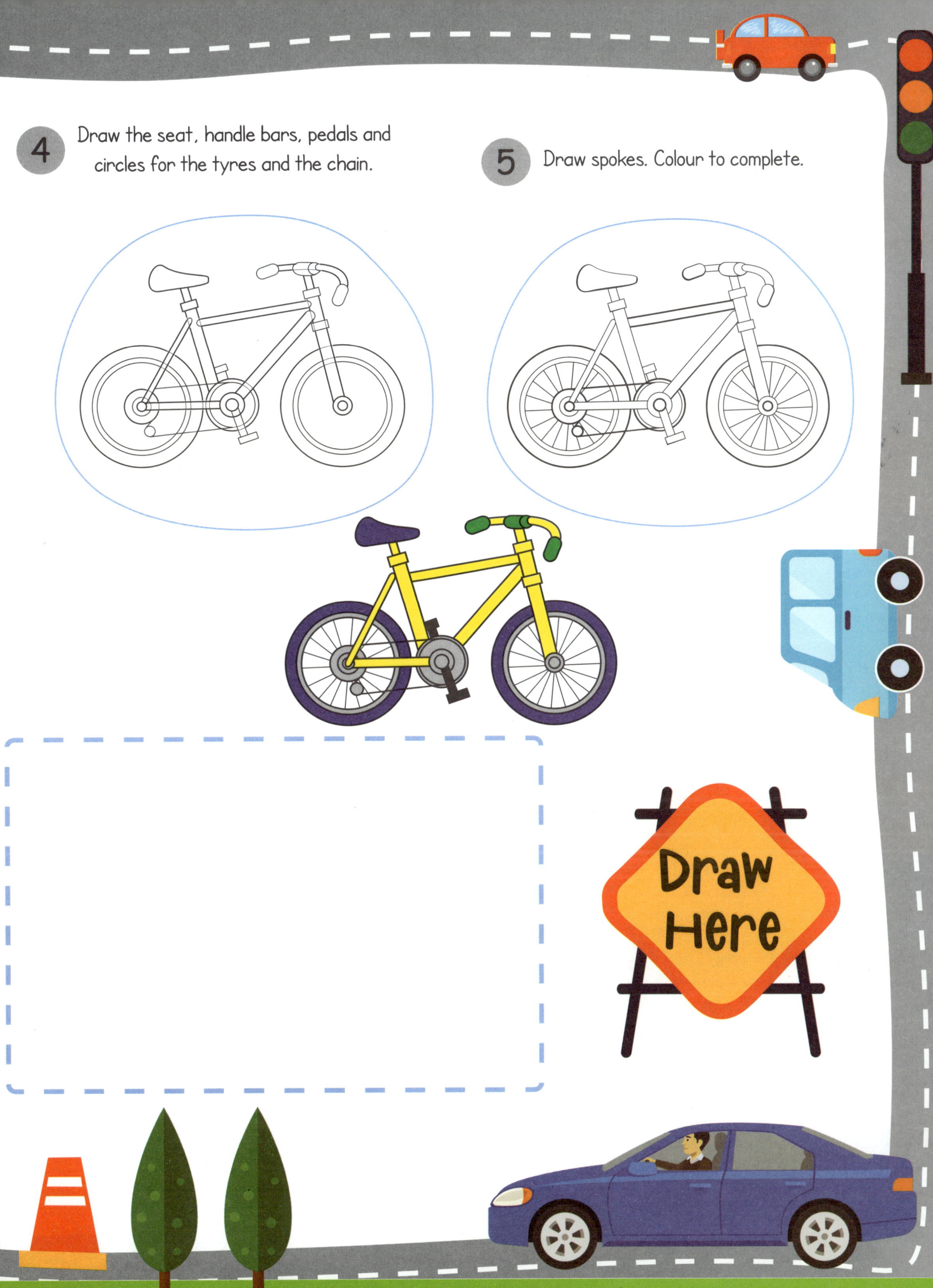
4
Draw the seat, handle bars, pedals and circles for the tyres and the chain.
5
Draw spokes. Colour to complete.
Draw Here

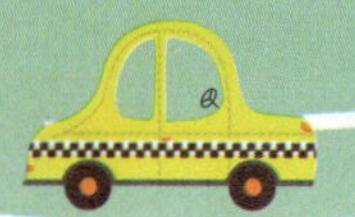

CAR

This is a car. It's a road vehicle that carries a small number of people.

1 Draw a rectangle with a big circle over it. Draw a small circle on the left. Draw another circle at the back, intersecting the big circle.

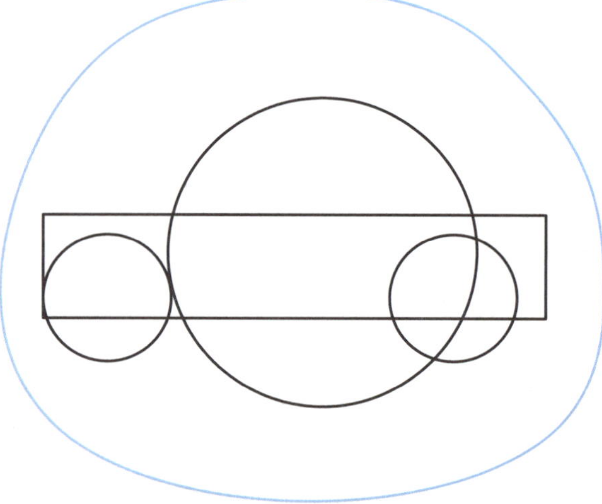

2 Draw a line from the middle of the rectangle, cutting the big circle.

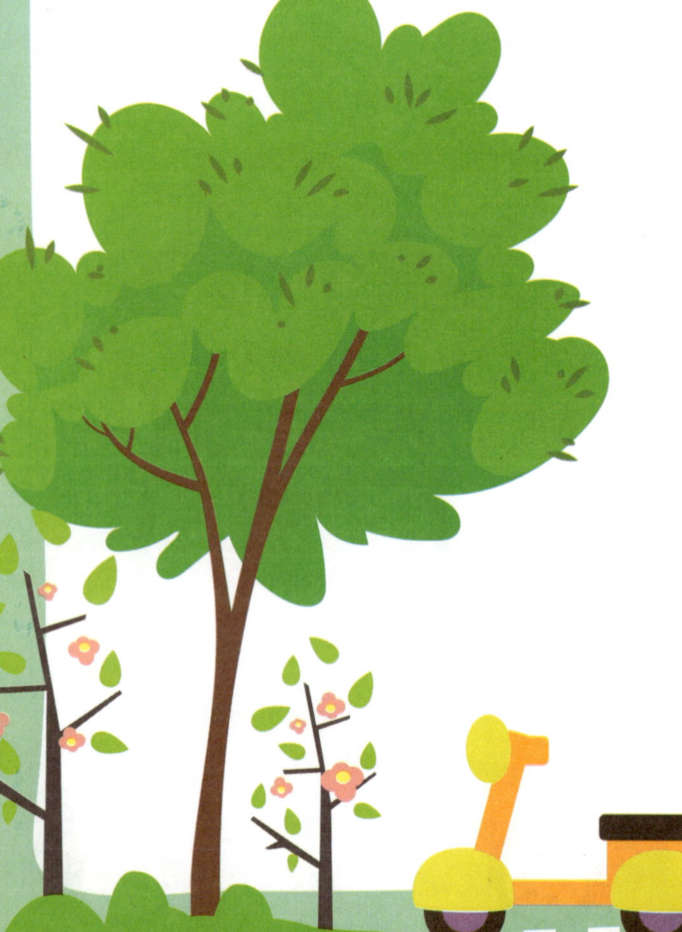

3 Draw circles for wheels. Draw a side mirror and a rectangle at the centre of the car roof

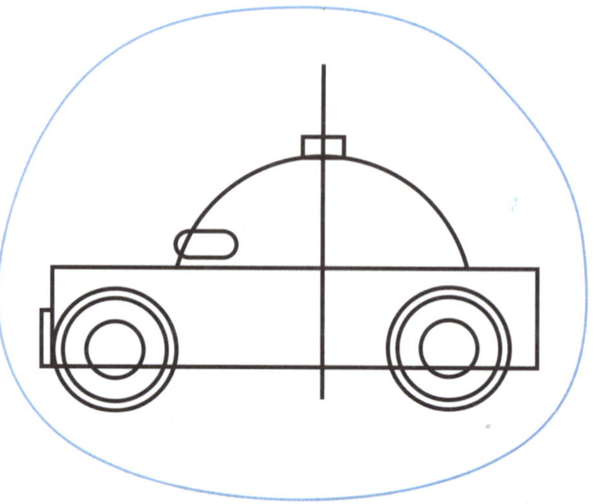

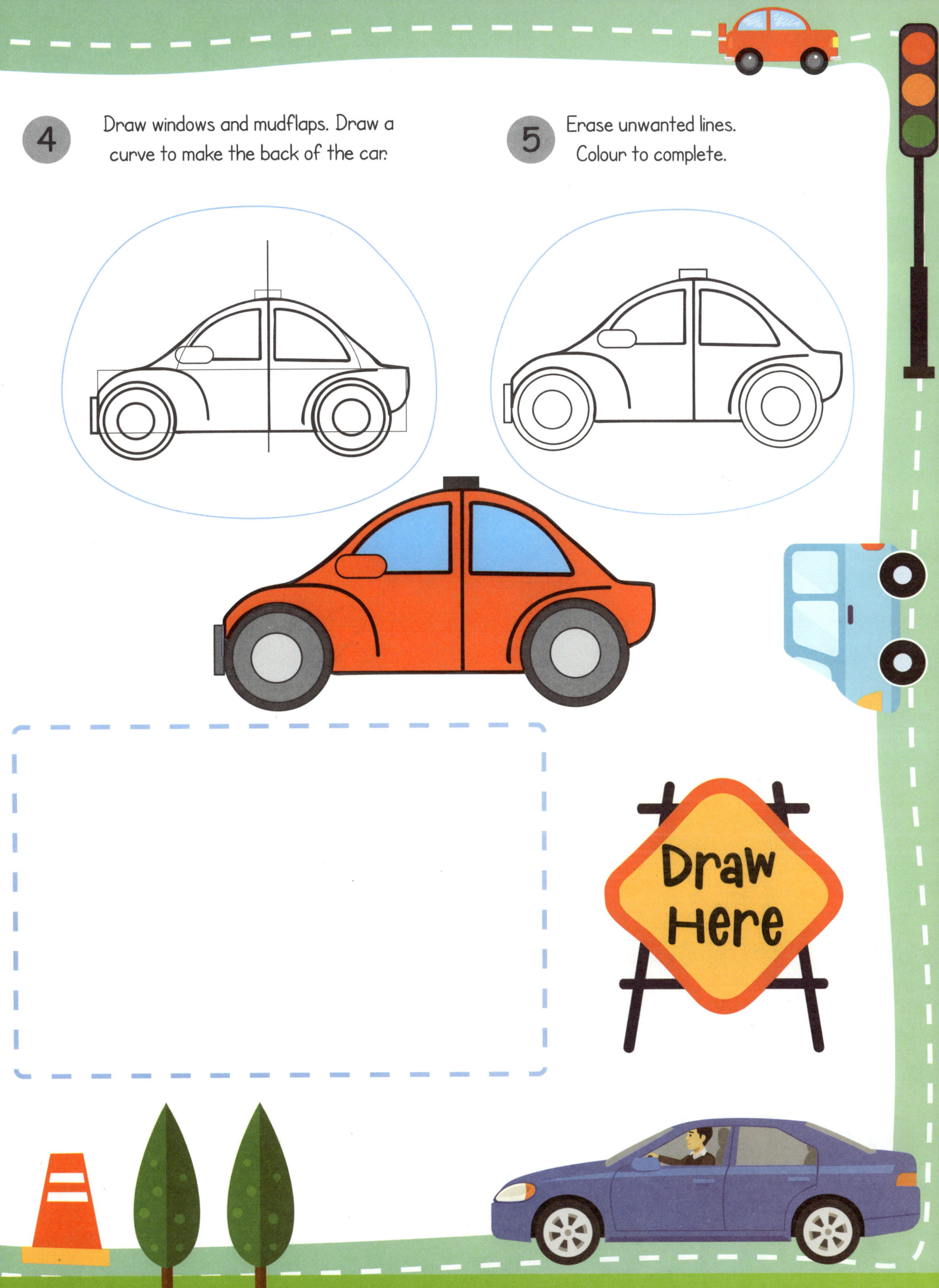
4
Draw windows and mudflaps. Draw a curve to make the back of the car.
5
Erase unwanted lines. Colour to complete.
Draw Here

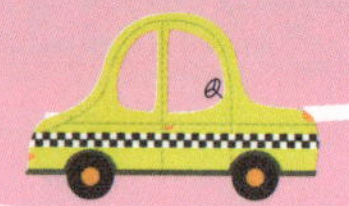

AIRPLANE

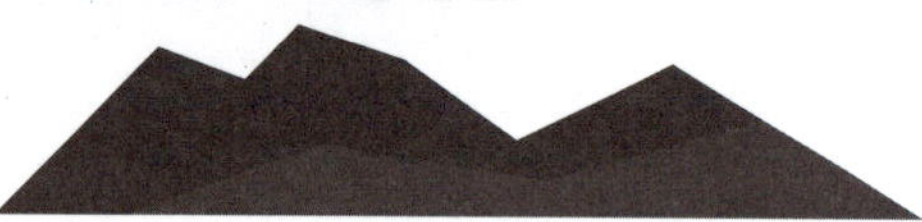

This is an airplane. It's a powered flying vehicle with fixed wings.

1 Draw an oval shape for the body. Draw the wing and tail of the plane.

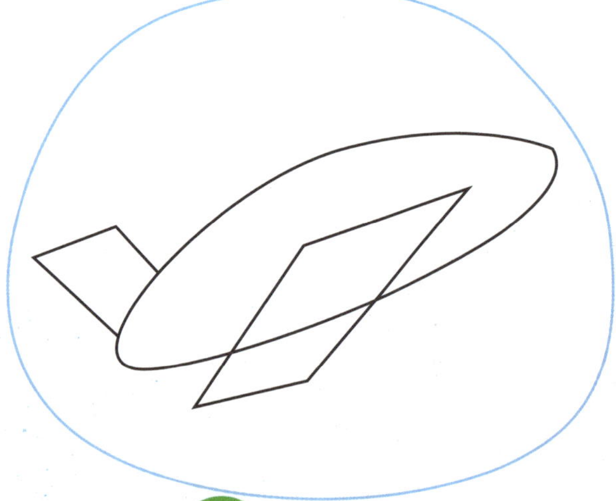

2 Curve the upper part to form the plane's front. Draw a circle above the curve. Erase unwanted lines.

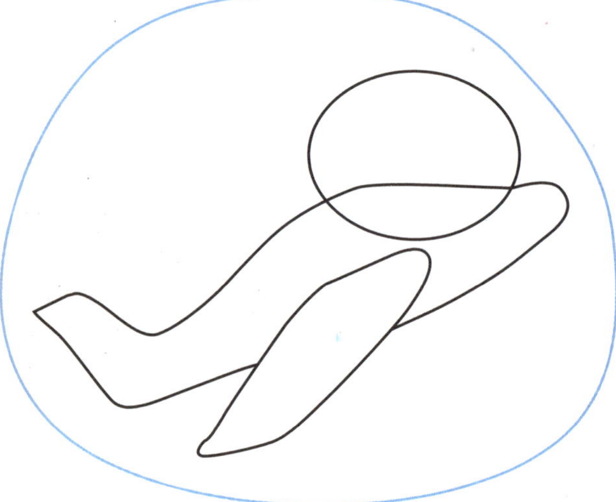

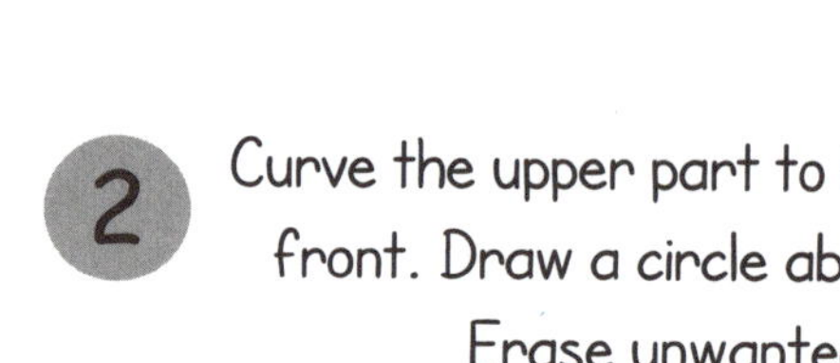

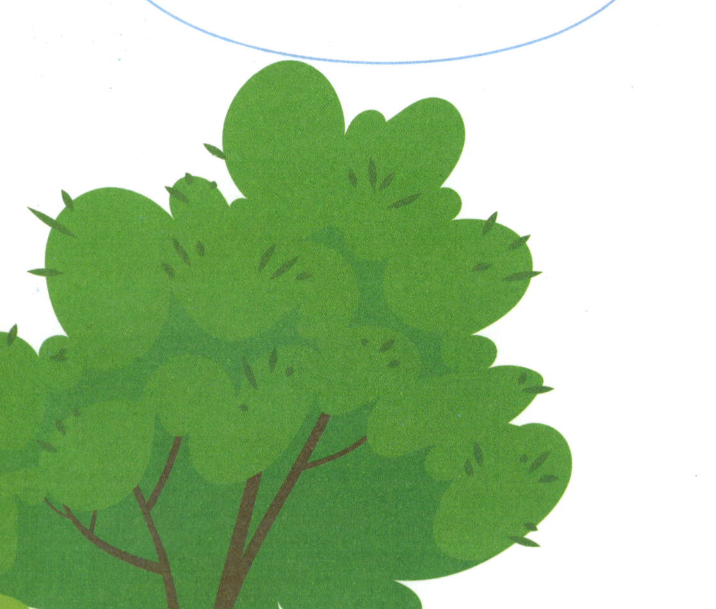

3 Draw a circle in the middle of the plane's body. Draw a line at the end of the wing.

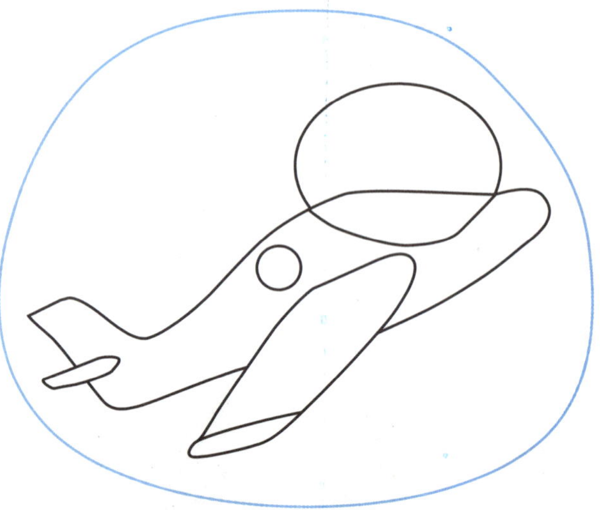

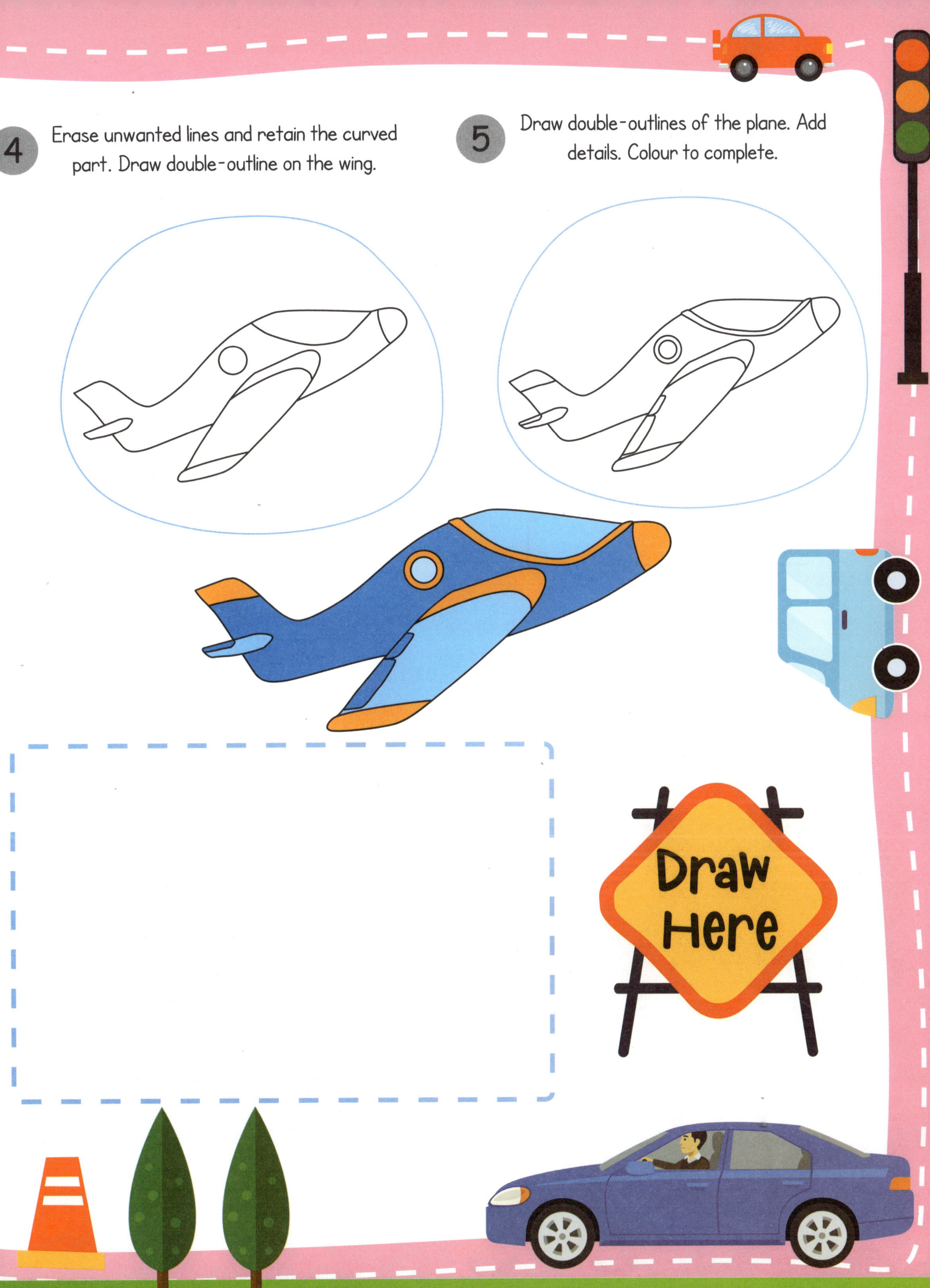
4
Erase unwanted lines and retain the curved part. Draw double-outline on the wing.
5
Draw double-outlines of the plane. Add details. Colour to complete.
Draw Here

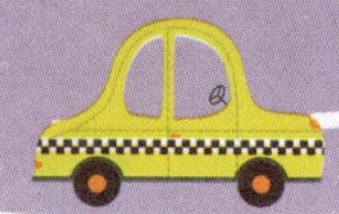

ENGINE

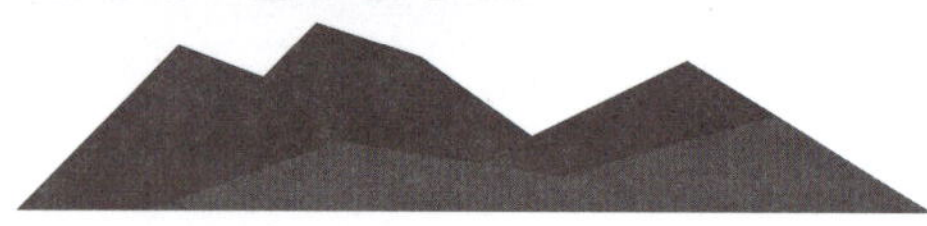

A train engine pulls a chain of interconnected carriages on steel train tracks.

1 Draw a rectangle.

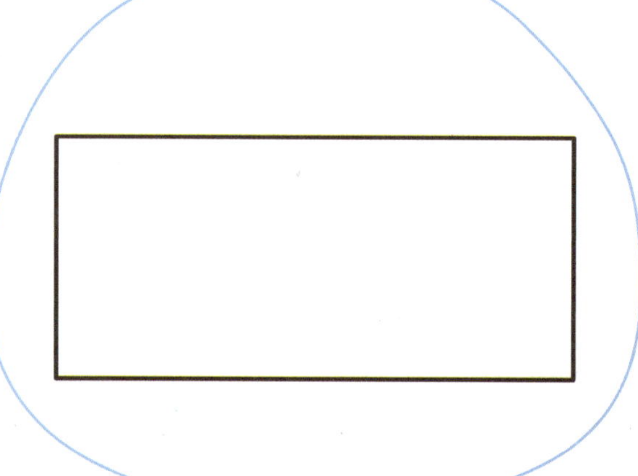

2 Curve the rectangle at the top left side. Draw three circles at the bottom of the square.

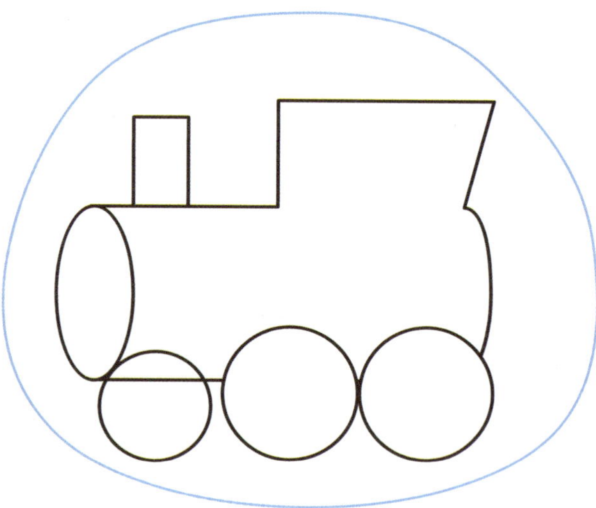

3 Draw windows. Erase unwanted lines.

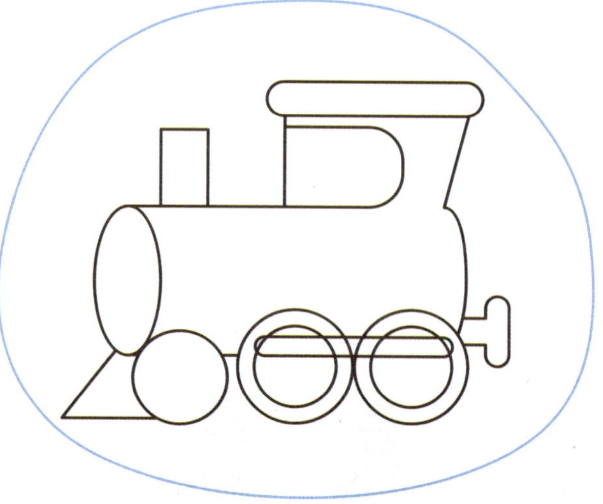

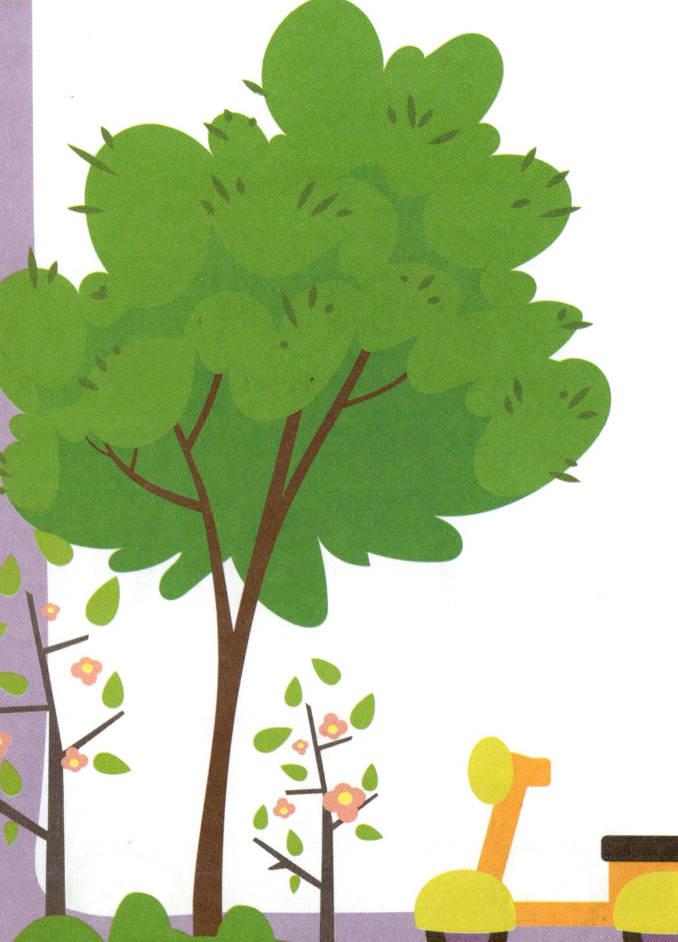

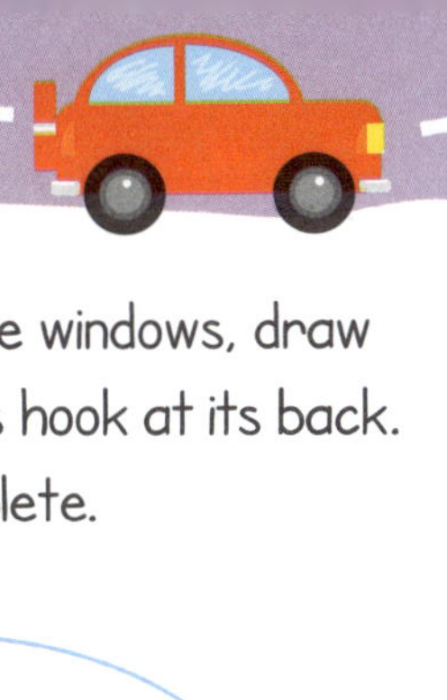

4 Draw double outlines over the wheels. Draw a cylindrical bar above the wheels.

5 Draw a roof rail. Below the windows, draw three lines. Draw the train's hook at its back. Colour to complete.

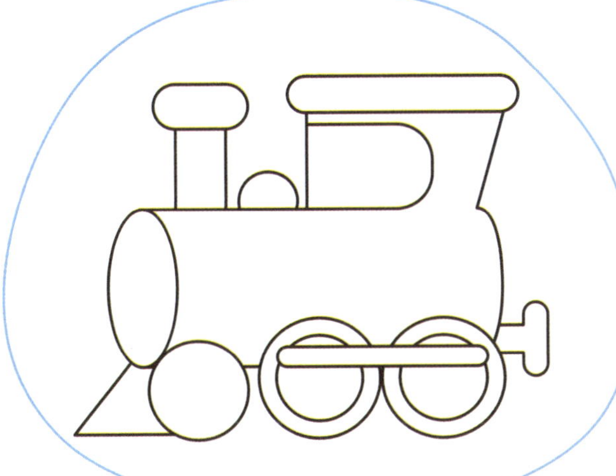

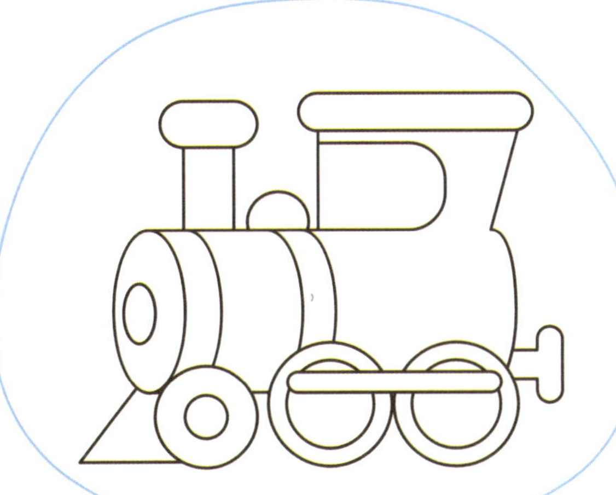

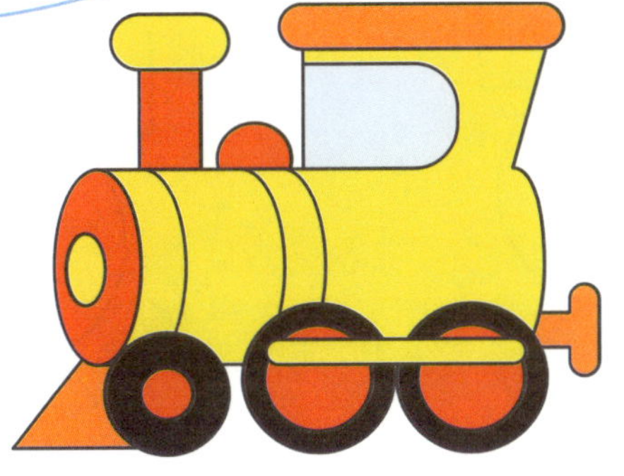

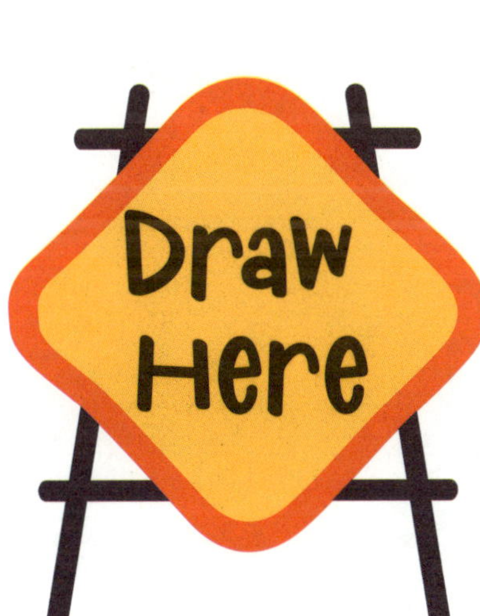

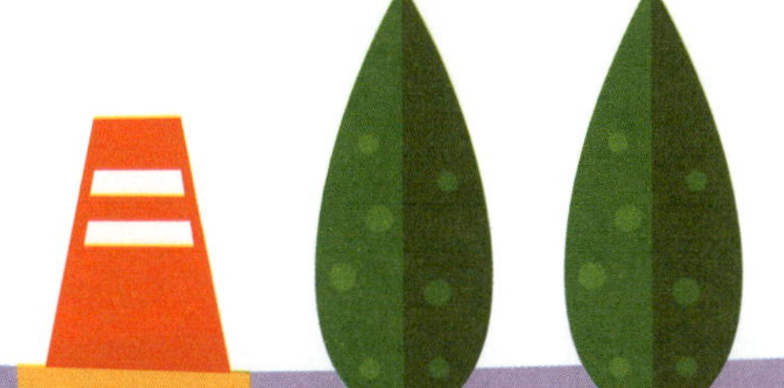

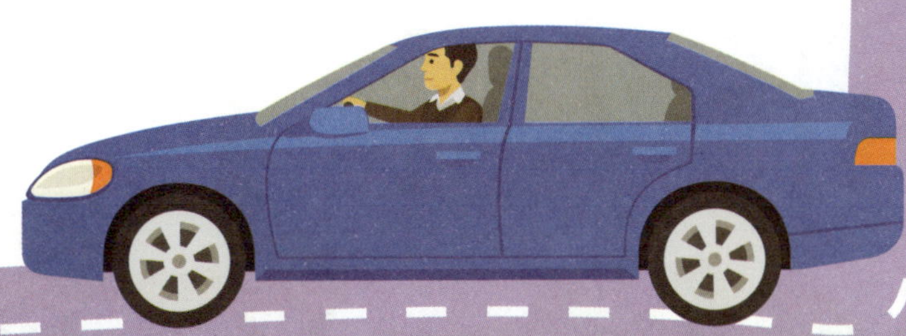

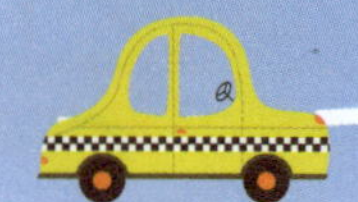

MONSTER TRUCK

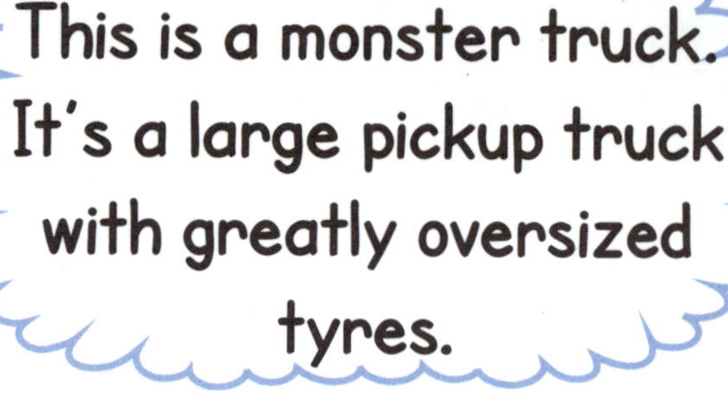

1 Draw two squares of slightly different sizes and a rectangle in a row. Draw two circles below for wheels.

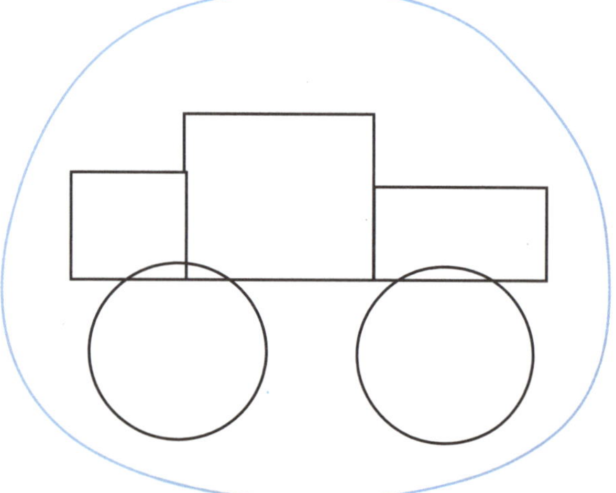

2 Draw details. Draw two bars above each tyre.

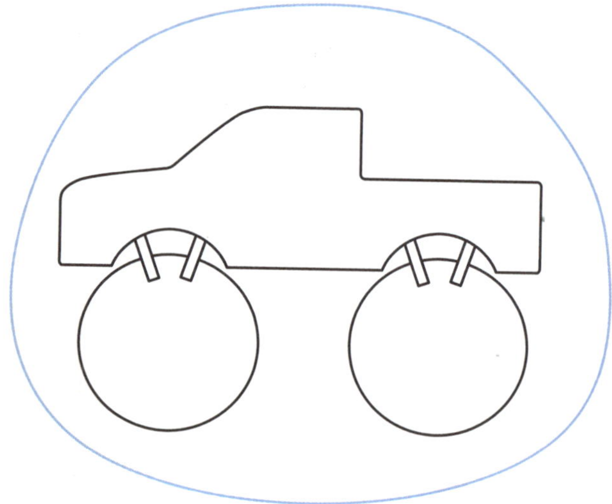

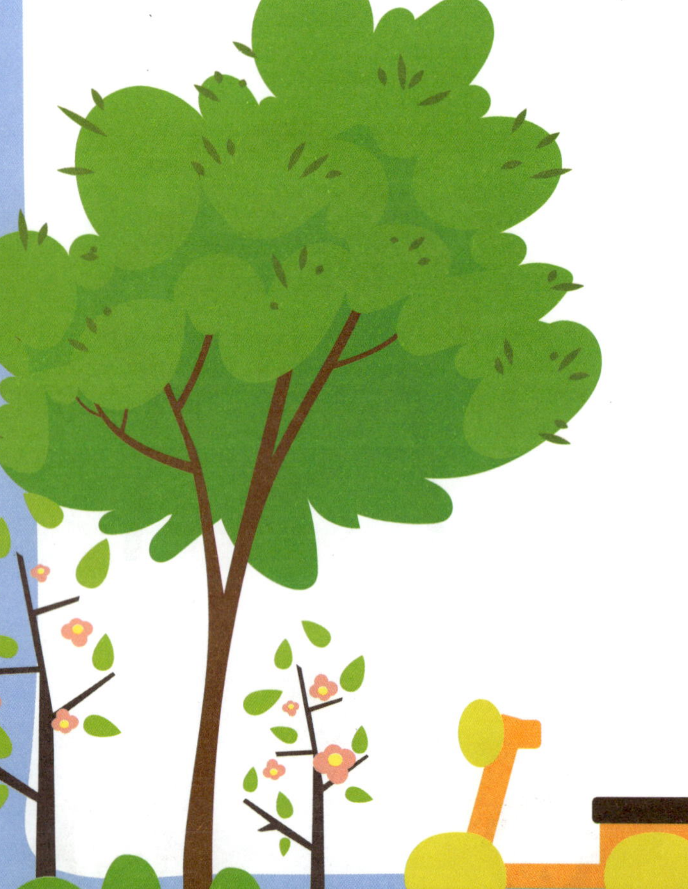

3 Draw small circles inside the wheels. Draw the lower front. Erase unwanted lines.

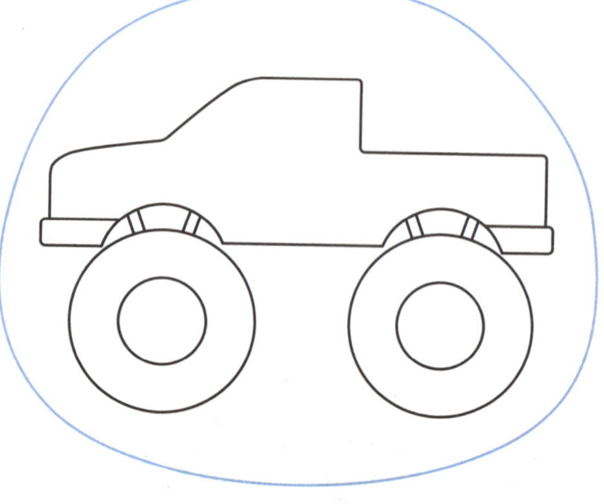

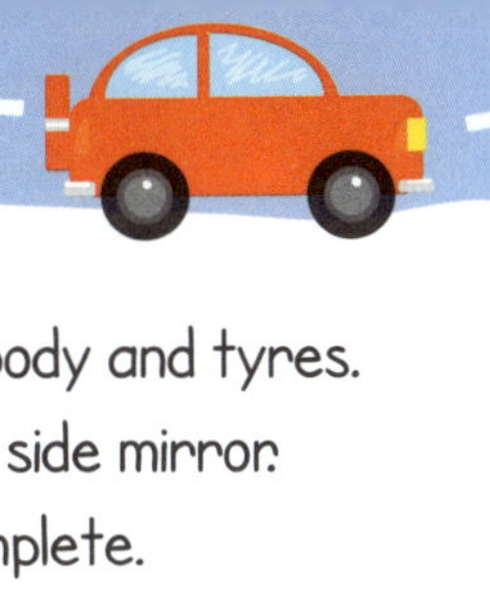

4 Draw windows. Draw two tiny circles for the wheels.

5 Draw designs on the body and tyres. Draw a light and a side mirror. Colour to complete.

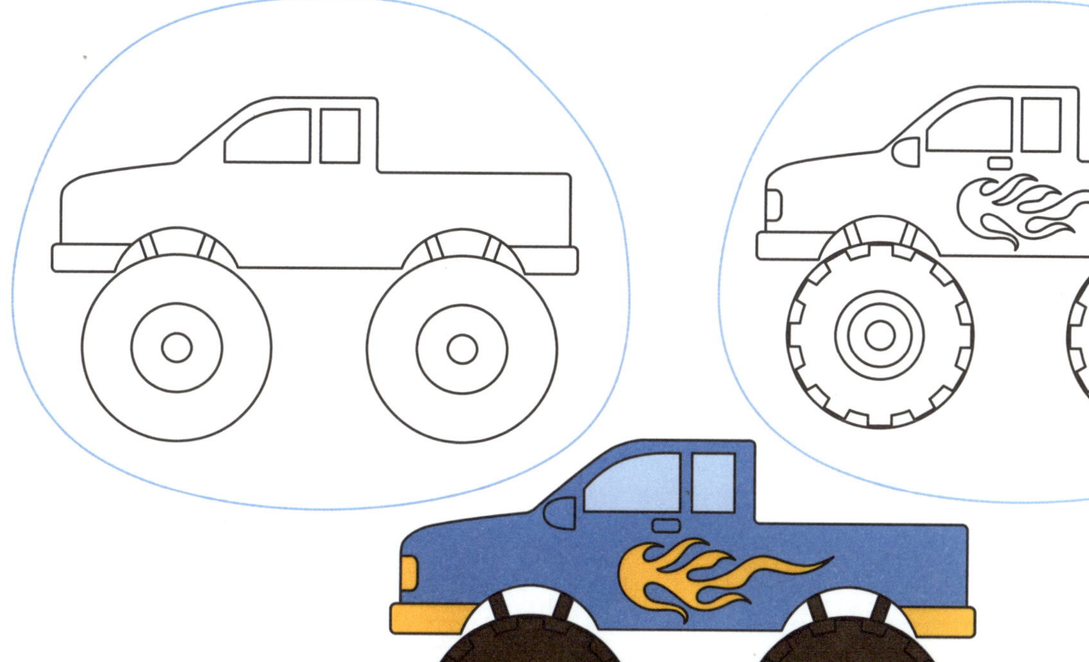

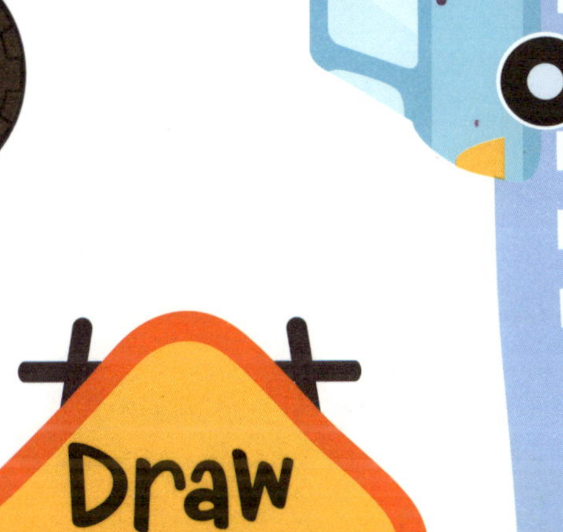

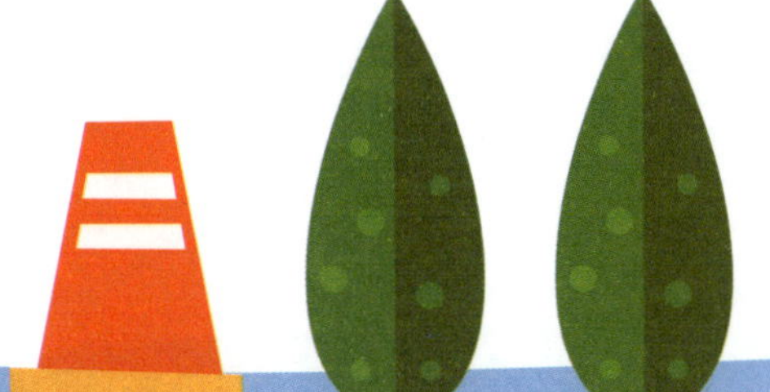

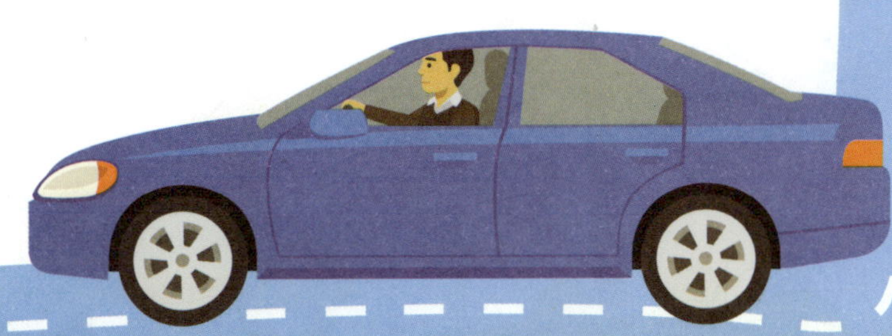

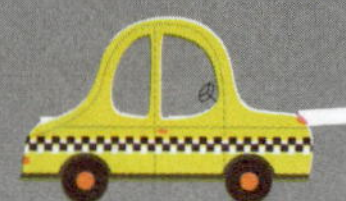

DUMP TRUCK

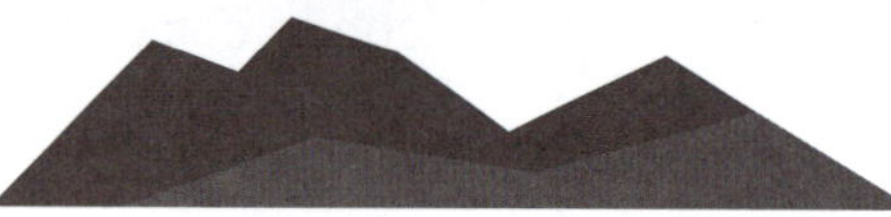

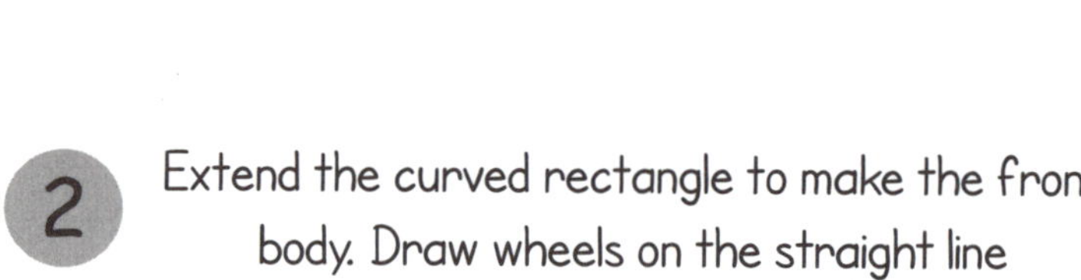

1 Draw a rectangle with curved ends joined to a bigger rectangle. Draw a straight line below them.

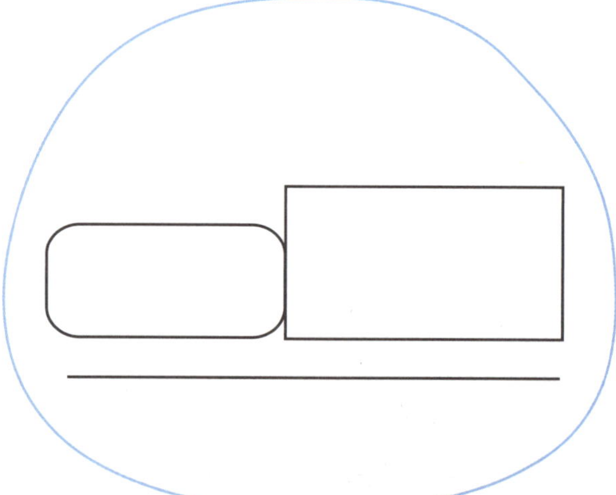

2 Extend the curved rectangle to make the front body. Draw wheels on the straight line intersecting the rectangles.

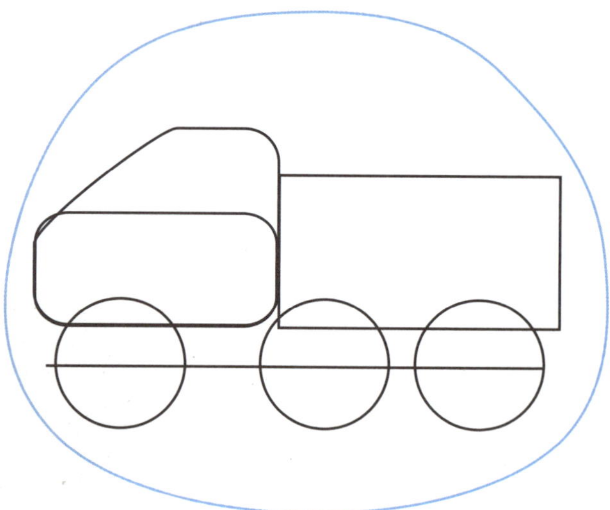

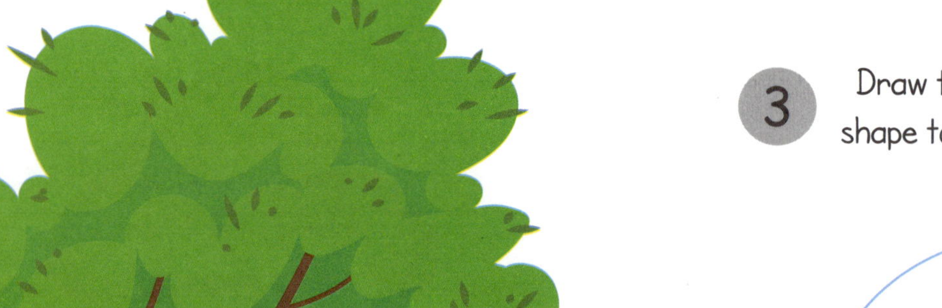

3 Draw the mud mound and details to give shape to the truck. Erase unwanted lines.

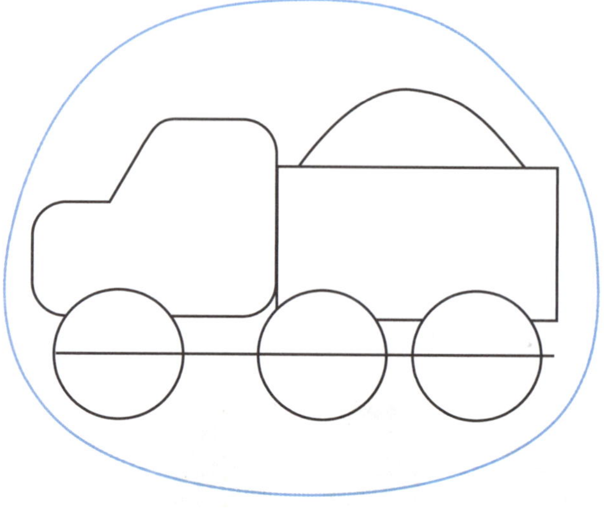

4 Draw circles inside the tyres, the head light, the windows and add mudflaps to the railings of the truck.

5 Draw the windows. Erase unwanted lines. Colour to complete.

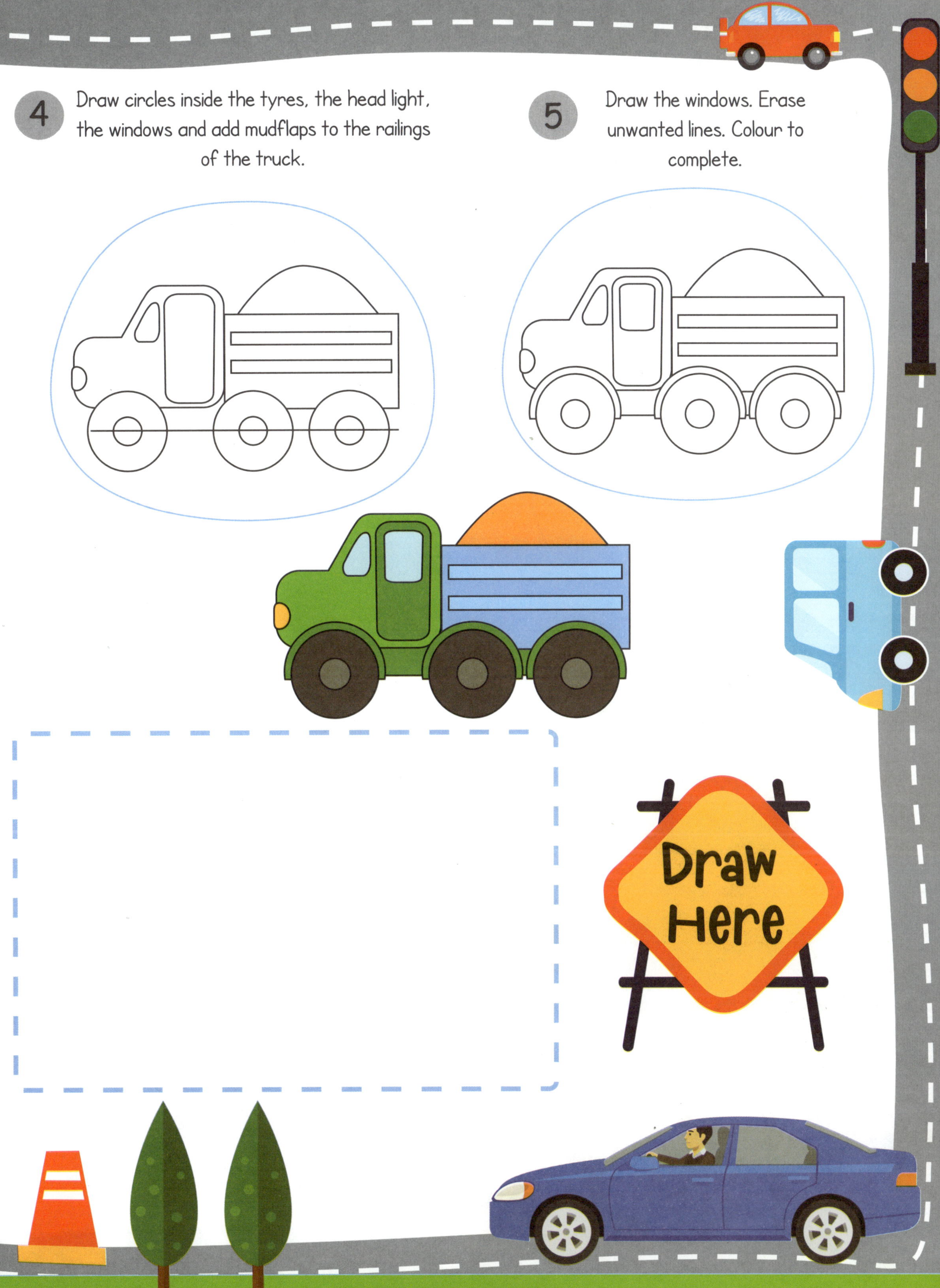

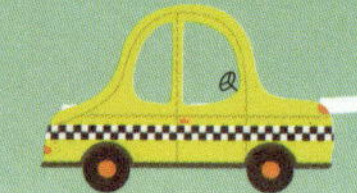

HOT AIR BALLOON

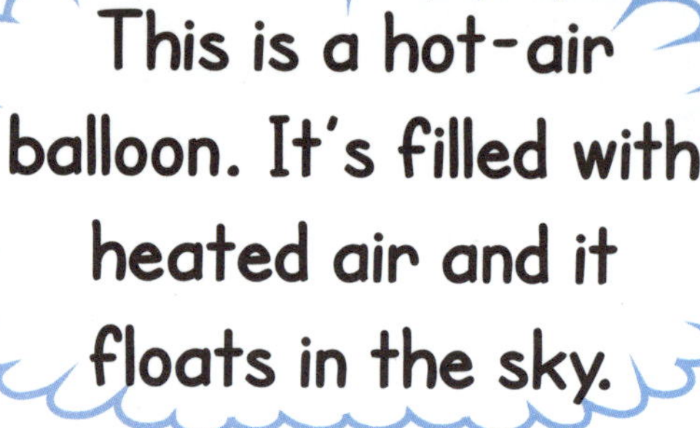

1 Draw a big circle for the body and a curved shape at the bottom of the circle.

2 Draw curved lines inside the circle until the bottom.

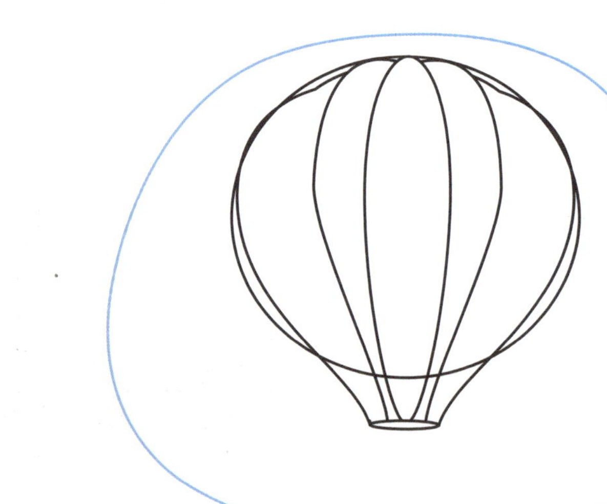

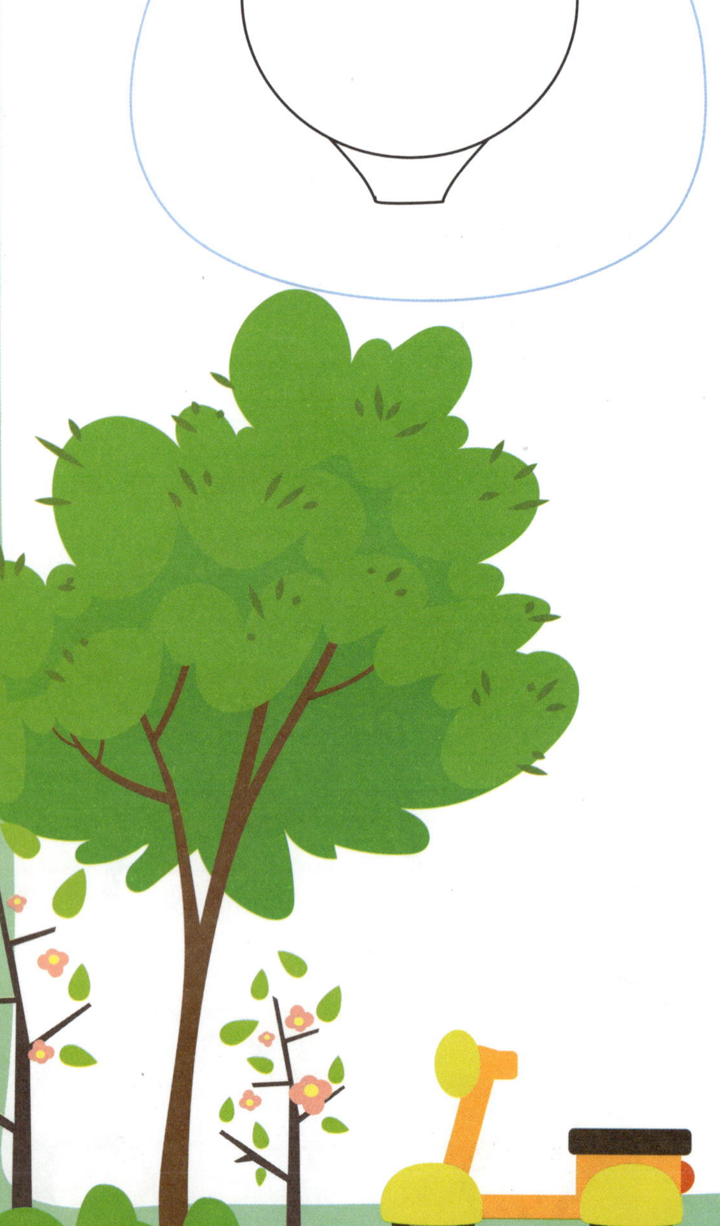

3 Draw a basket at the bottom for the seating part. Erase unwanted lines.

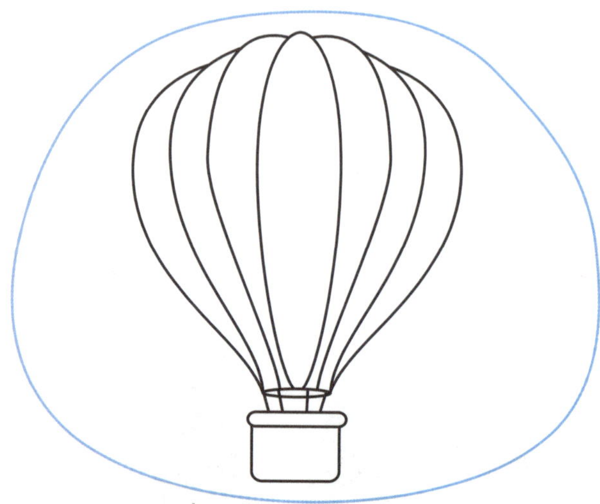

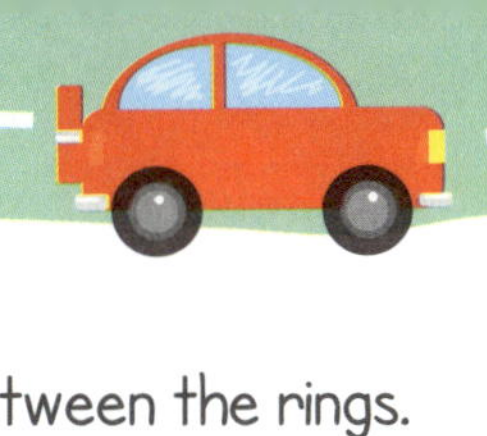

4 Draw rings above the basket. Draw a bulb-shaped design on the basket.

5 Draw the design between the rings. Colour to complete.

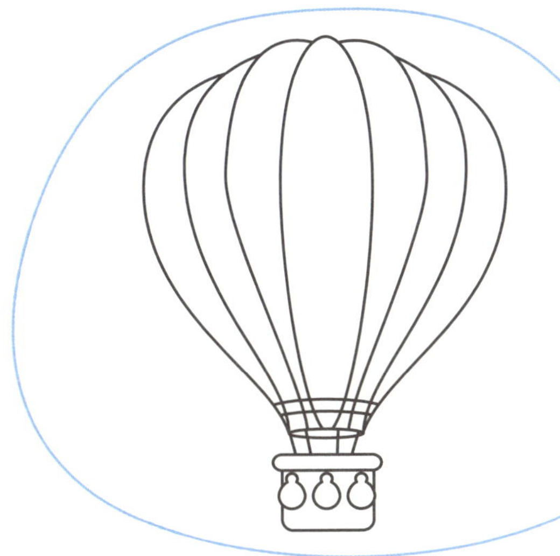

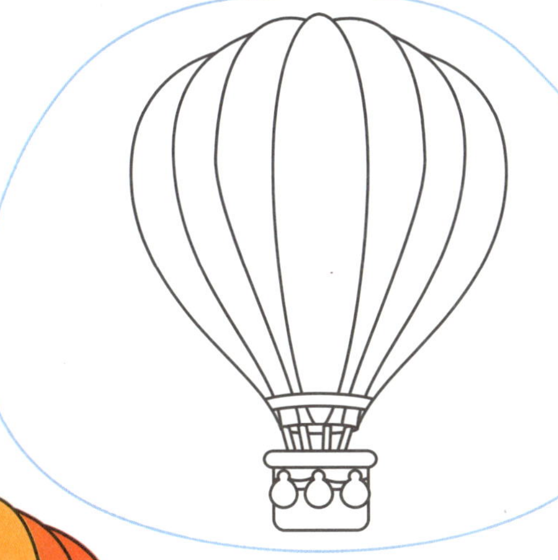

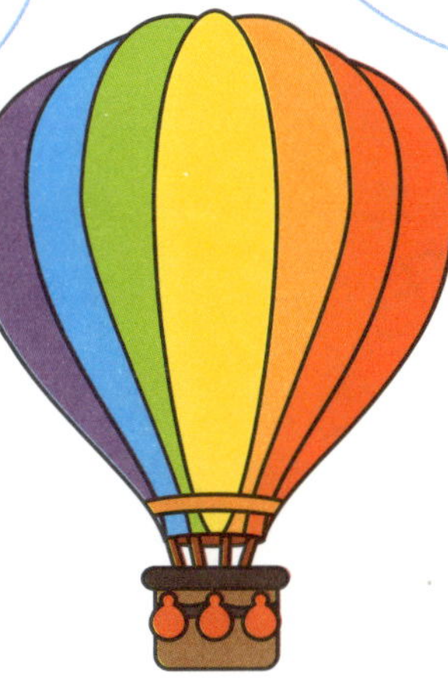

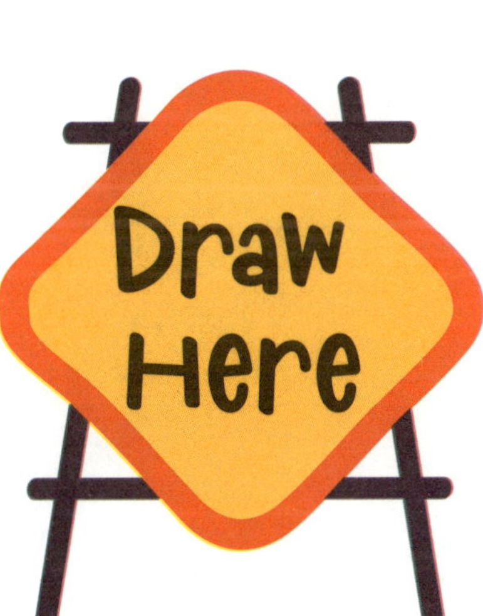

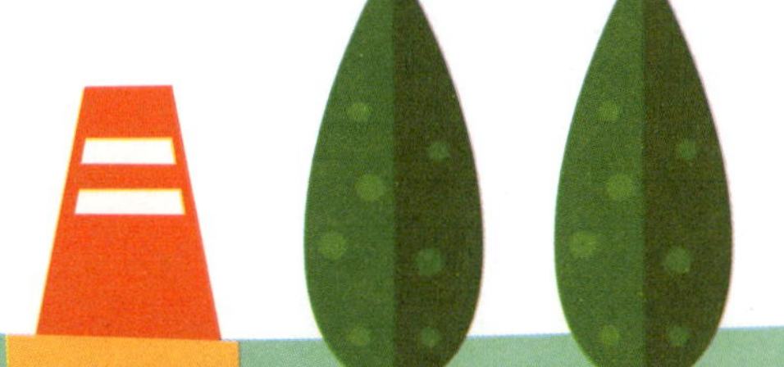

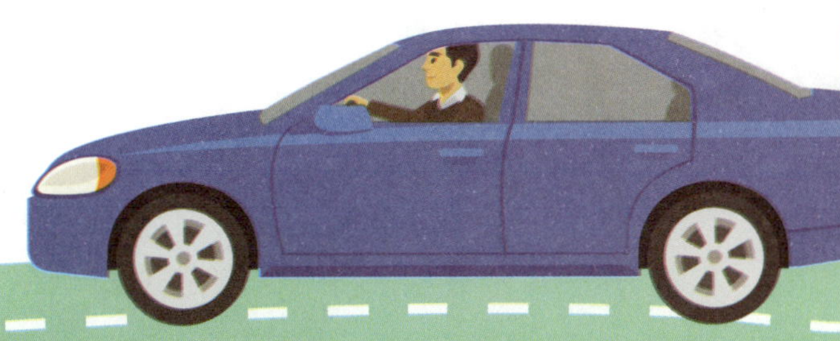

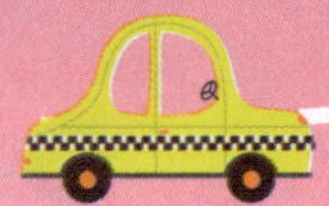

STEAMSHIP

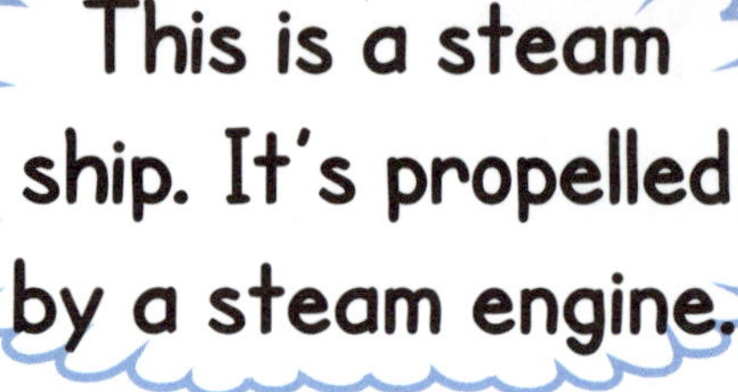

1. Draw three boat shapes one above the other.

2. Curve each boat shape to form the body. Draw a curved shape for smoke.

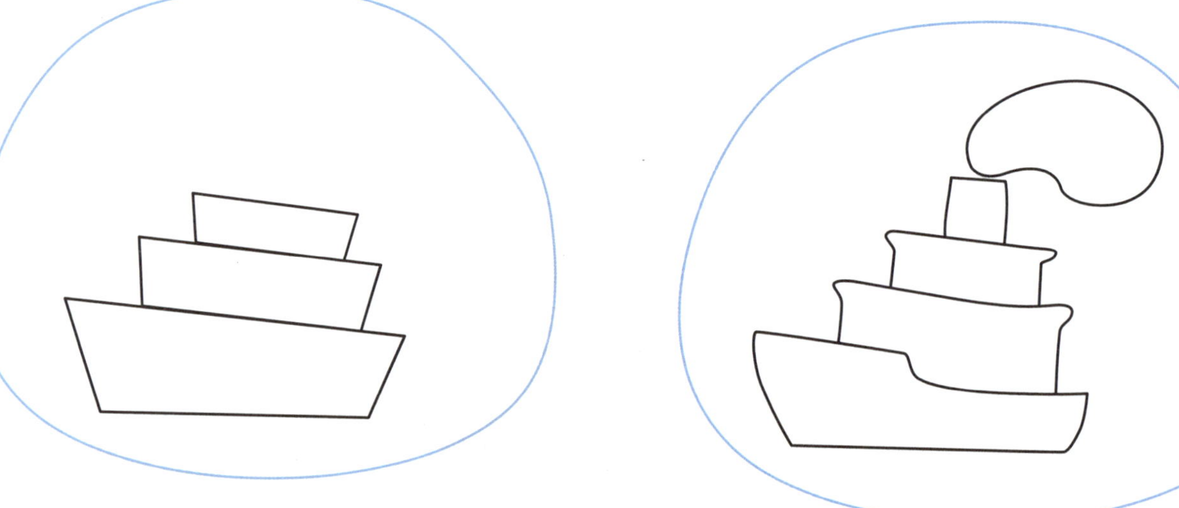

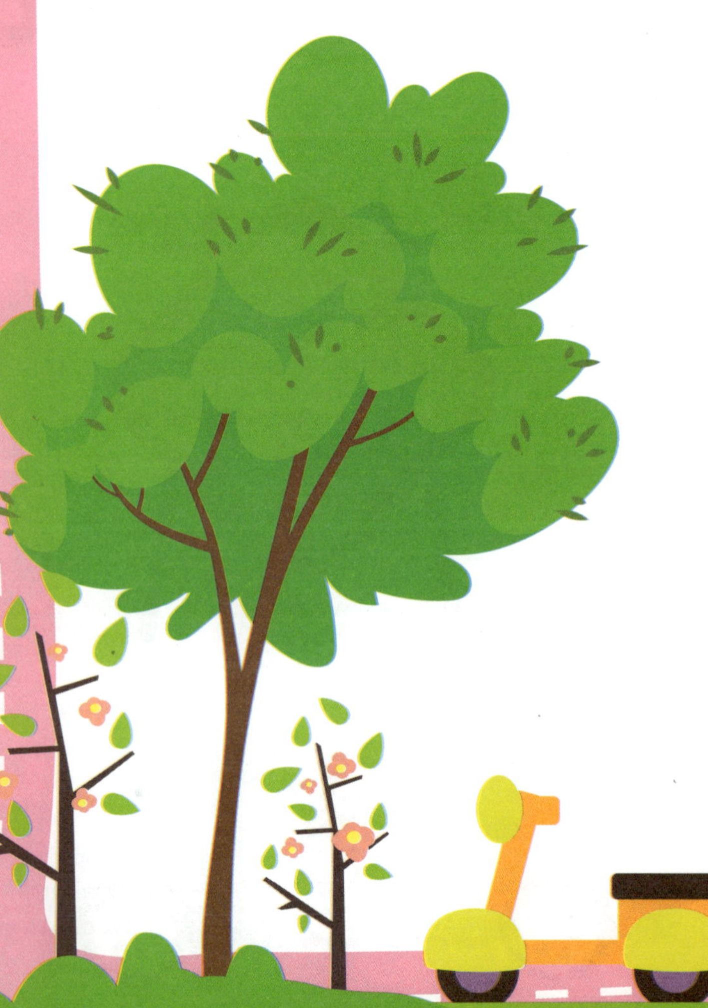

3. Draw a cylinder shape over the topmost boat shape. Draw details to make the smoke bubble.

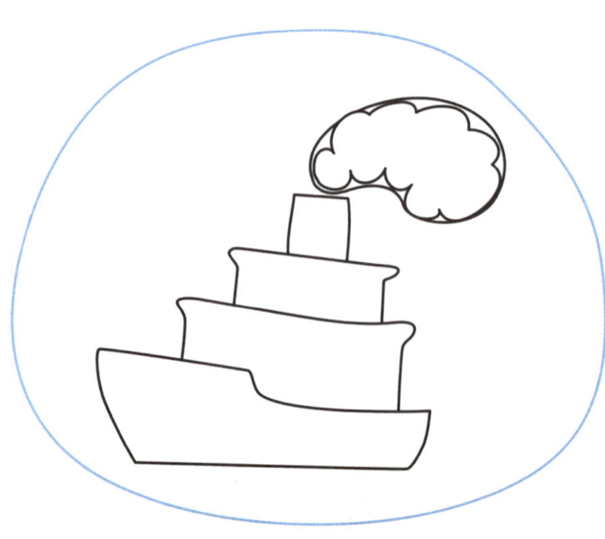

4 Erase unwanted lines. Draw the water.

5 Draw lines at the top and circles for windows. Colour to complete.

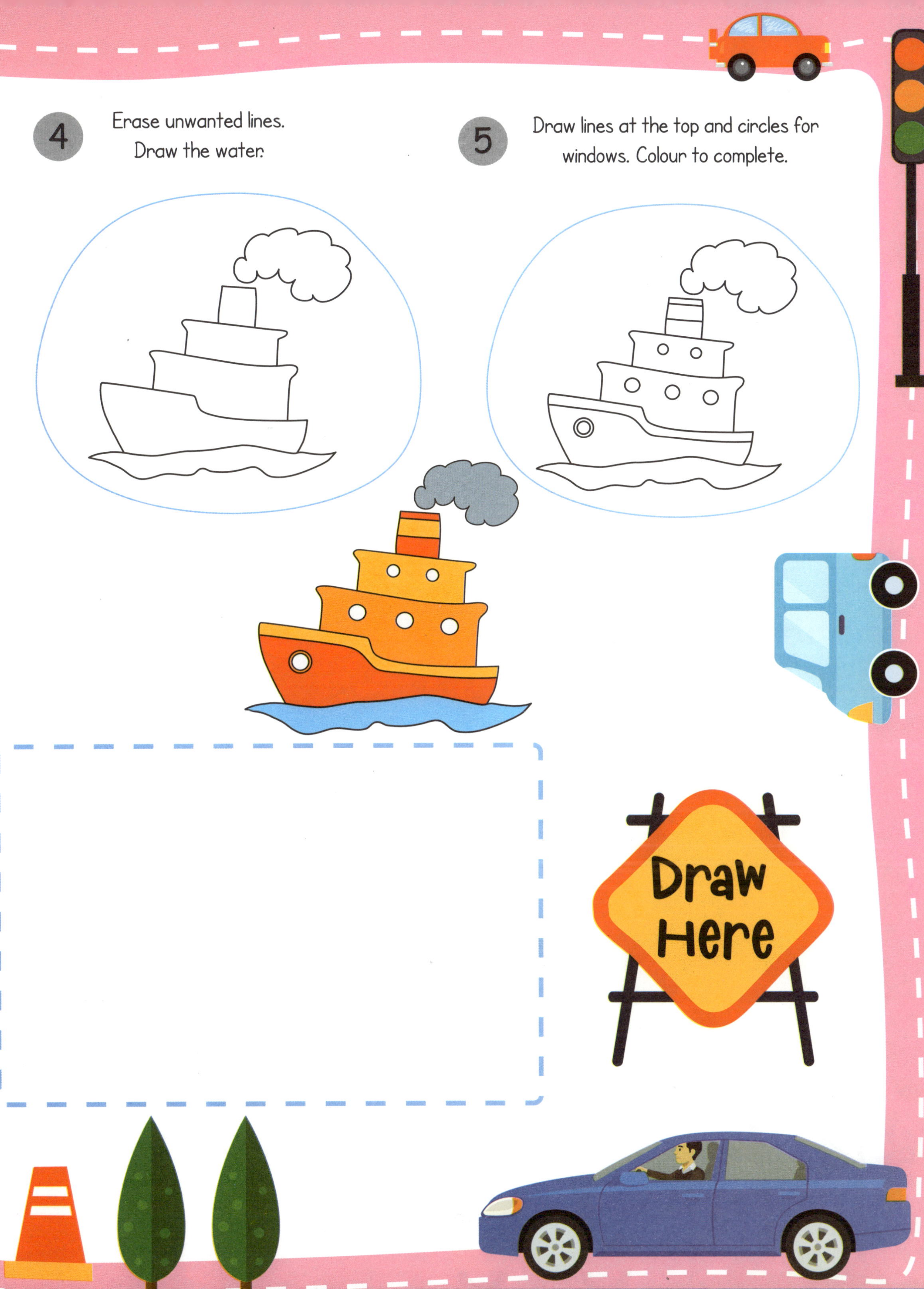

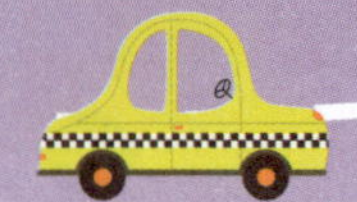

BUS

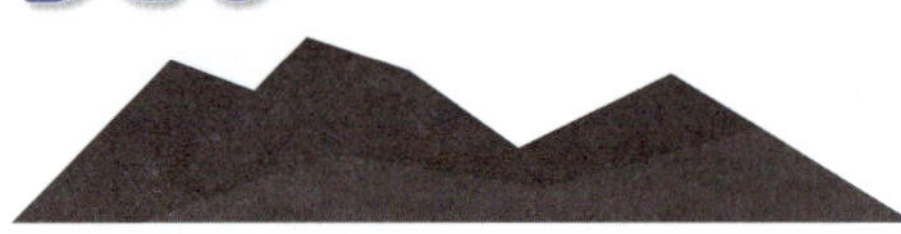

This is a bus. It's a large motor vehicle that carries passengers by road.

1 Draw a rectangle. On its right, extend the rectangle a little for the front body.

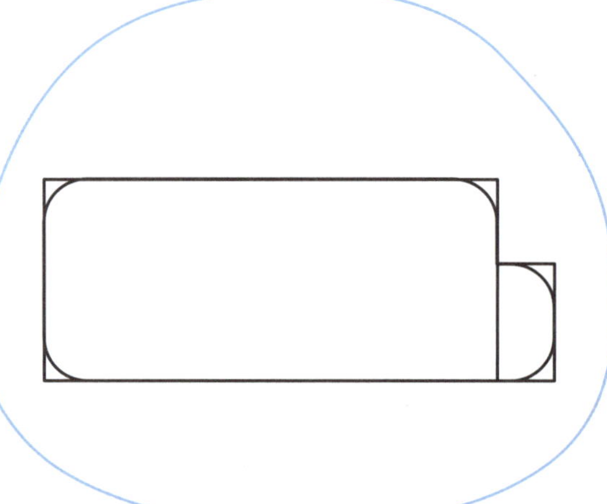

2 Curve all the corners and draw two circles for wheels.

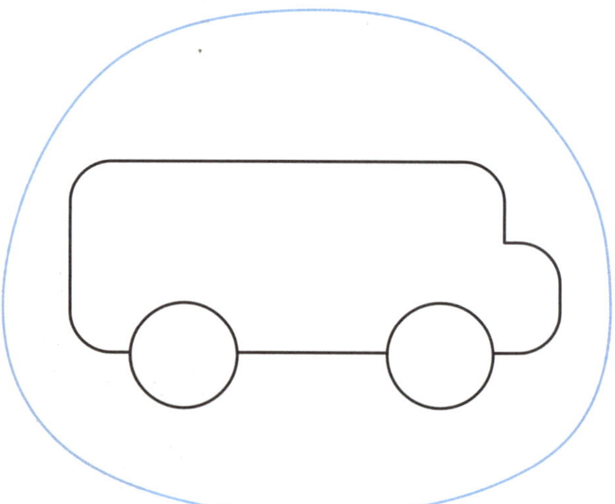

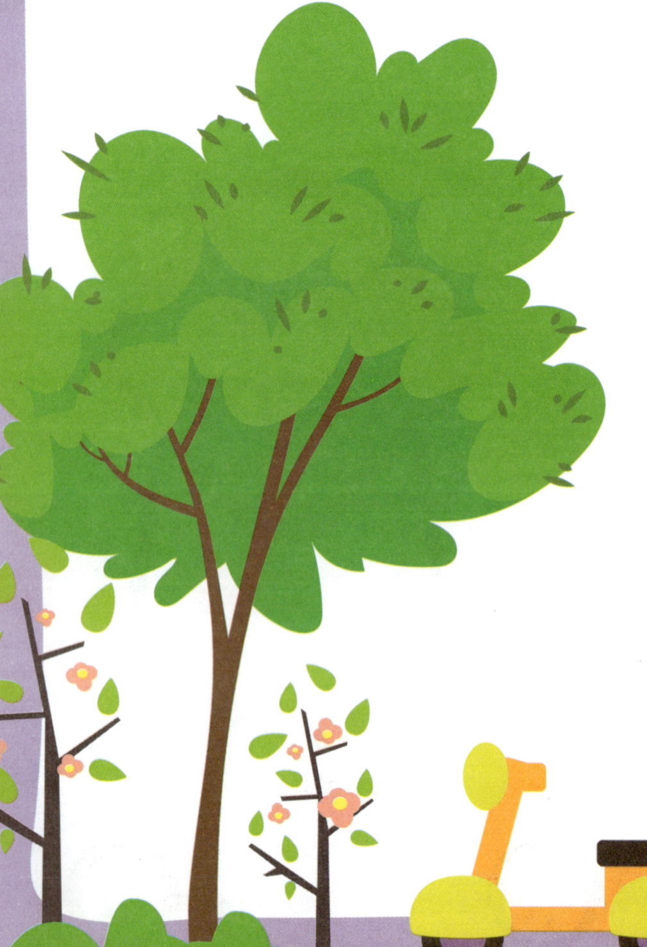

3 Draw circles inside the wheels and a window.

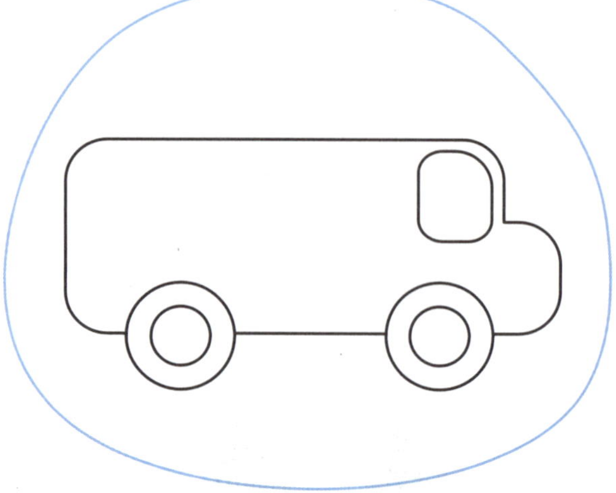

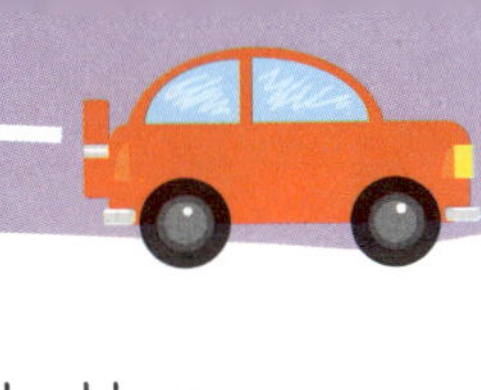

4 Draw mudflaps and windows on the bus.

5 Draw a front light and add minor details. Colour to complete.

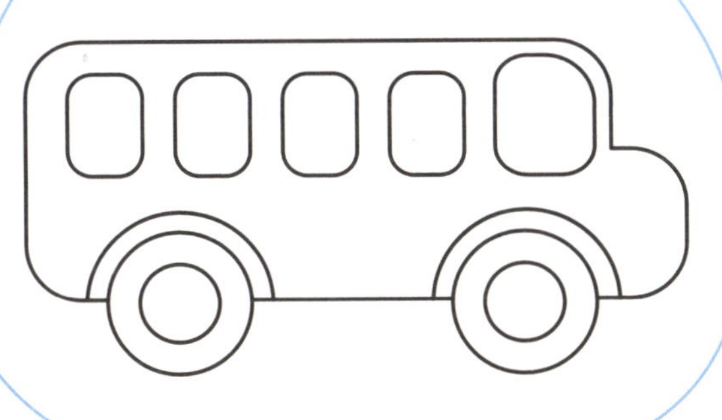

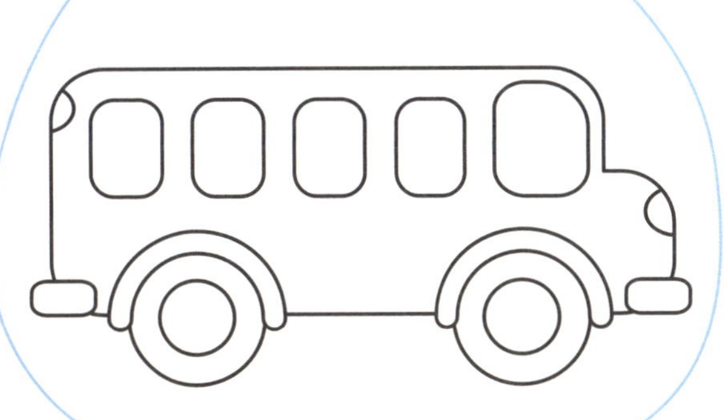

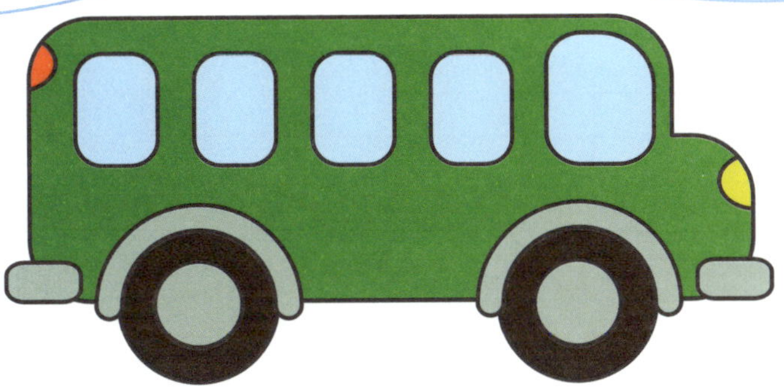

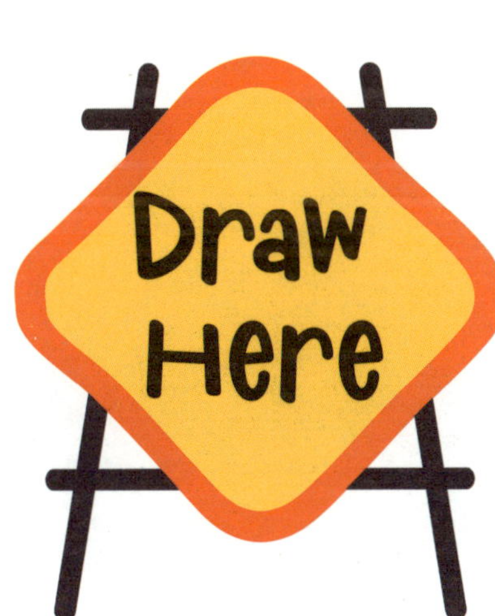

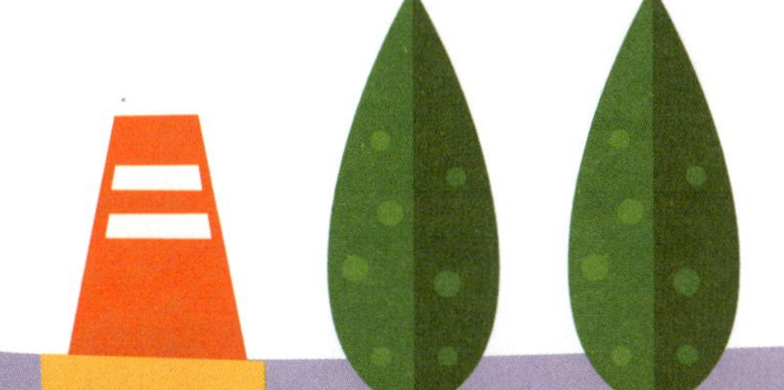

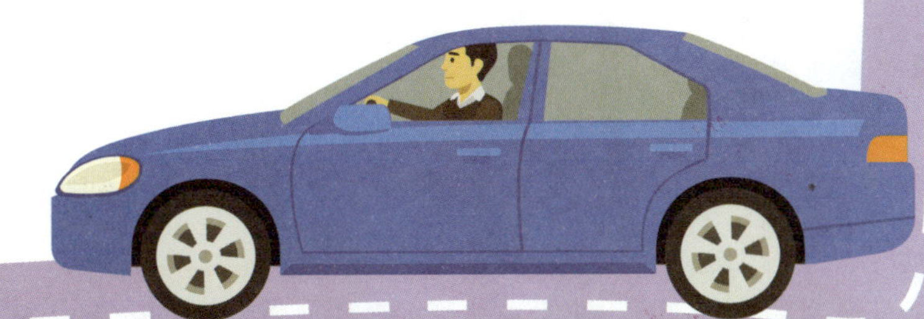

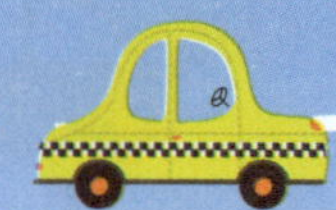

EXCAVATOR

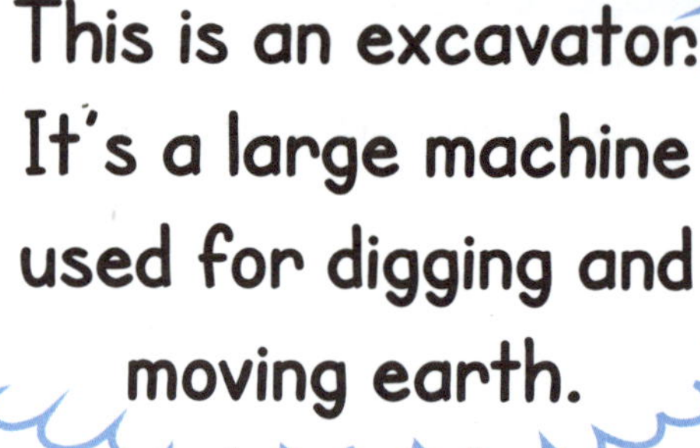

1 Draw a rectangle. Above it, make a square and a rectangle on the right side. Draw a curved cylinder shape at the top.

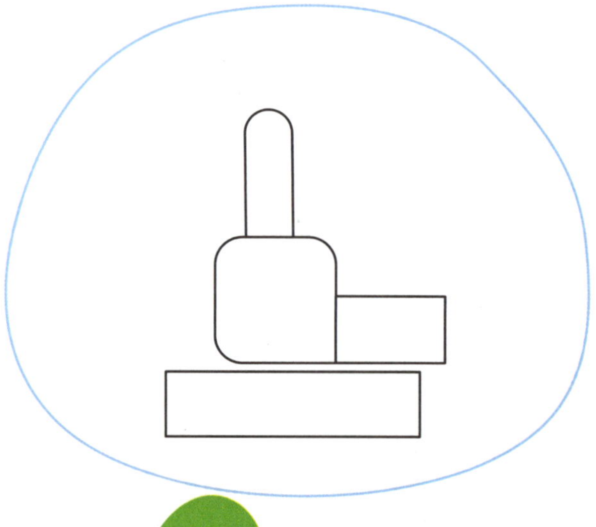

2 Draw lines at both ends of the rectangle at the bottom and the rectangle above. Draw another cylindrical shape on top of the existing cylinder.

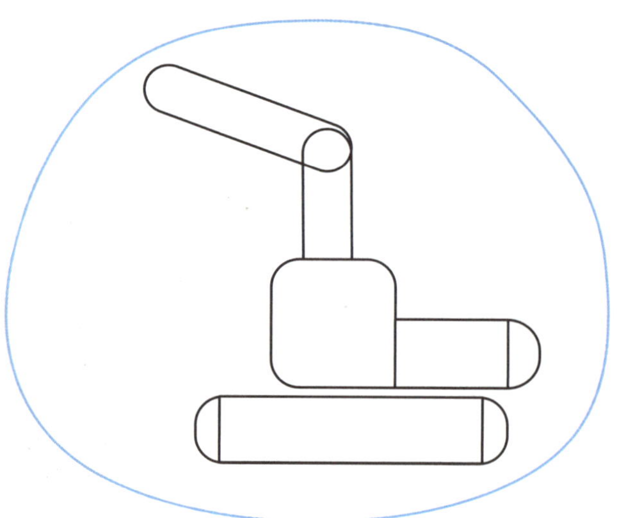

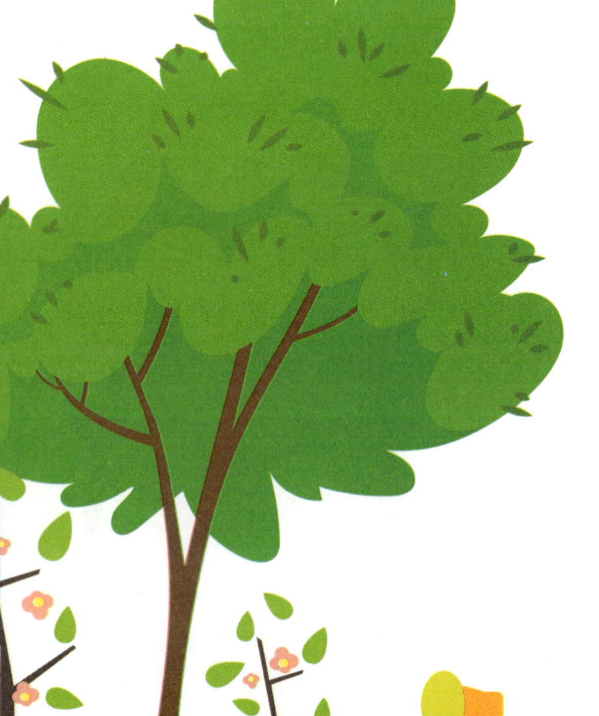

3 Draw the excavator's hand from the cylindrical shape. Draw two lines at the bottom of the rectangle. Erase unwanted lines.

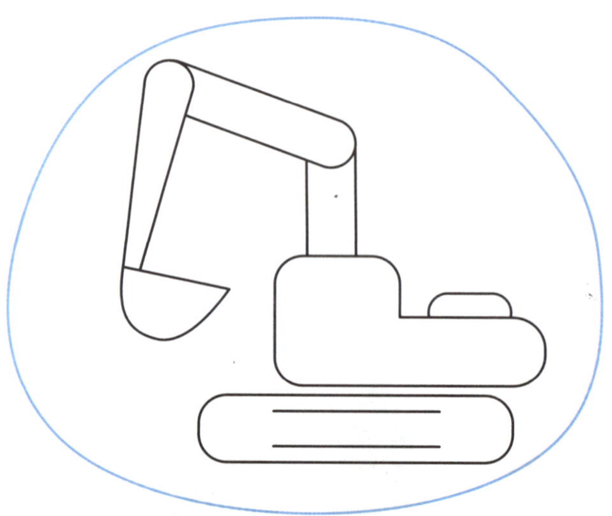

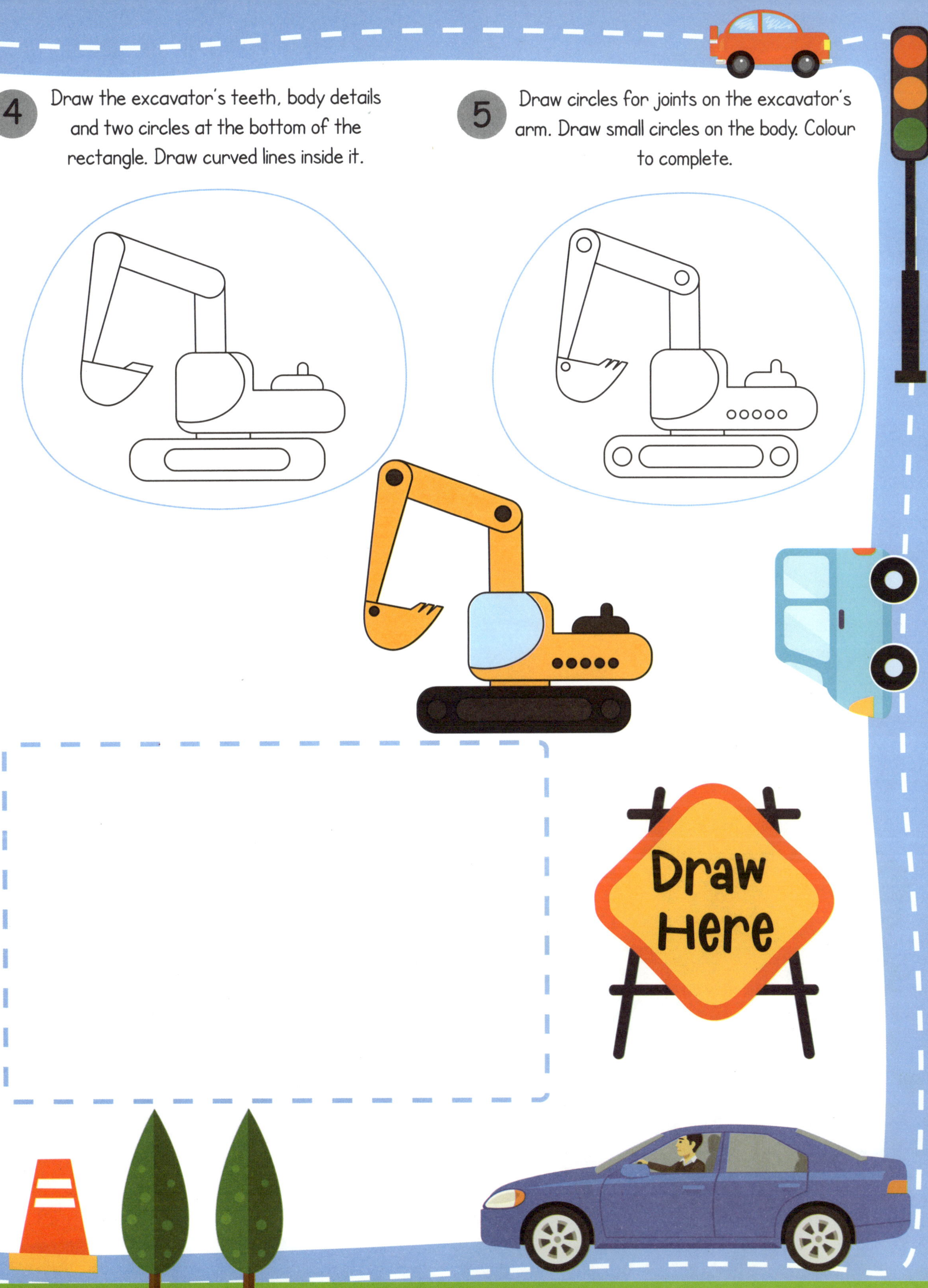
4
Draw the excavator's teeth, body details and two circles at the bottom of the rectangle. Draw curved lines inside it.
5
Draw circles for joints on the excavator's arm. Draw small circles on the body. Colour to complete.
Draw Here

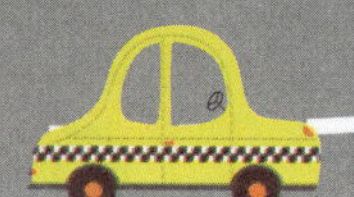

TIPPER TRUCK

This is a tipper truck. It has a rear platform that can be raised at its front end.

1 Draw two circles for wheels. Add lines for the front and back bodies.

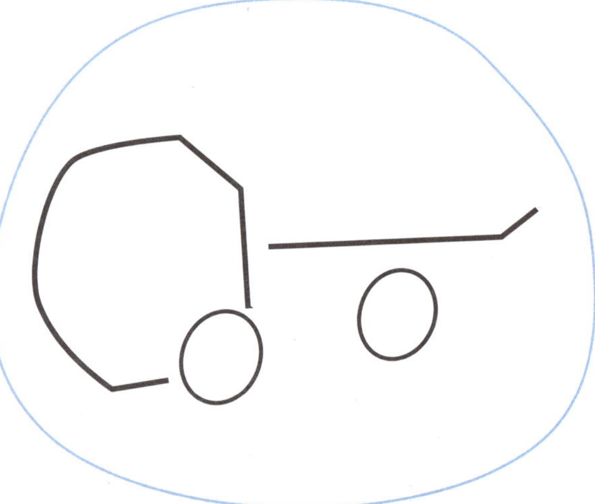

2 Draw more lines for the window and back part.

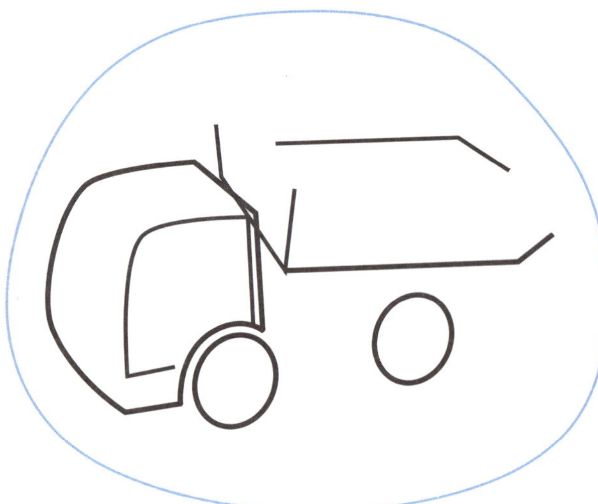

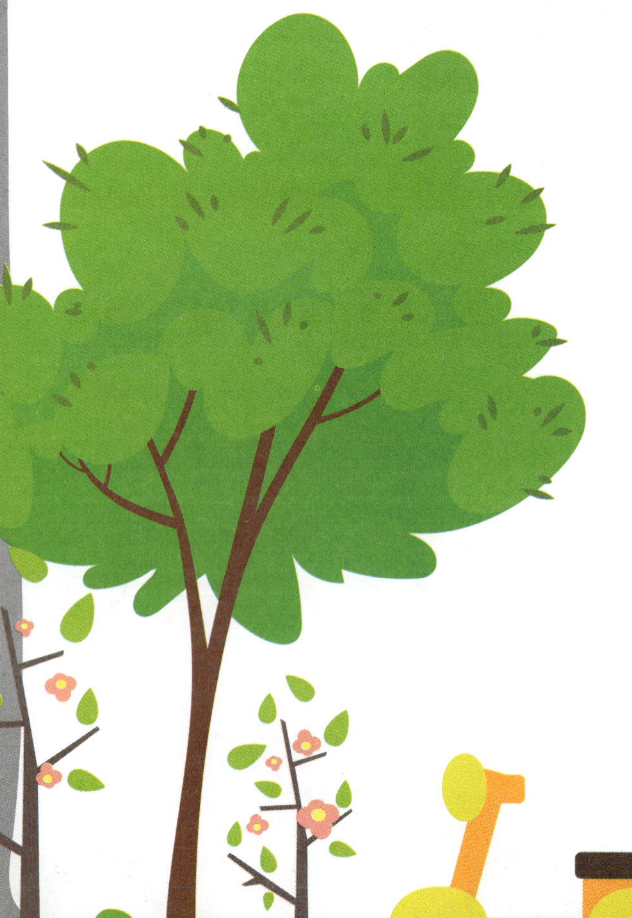

3 Draw the windshield, window, tyres and back body.

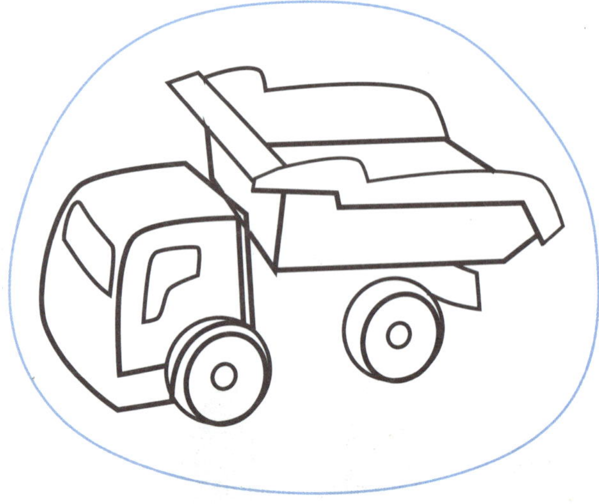

4 Draw lights, a box between the tyres and other details.

5 Colour to complete.

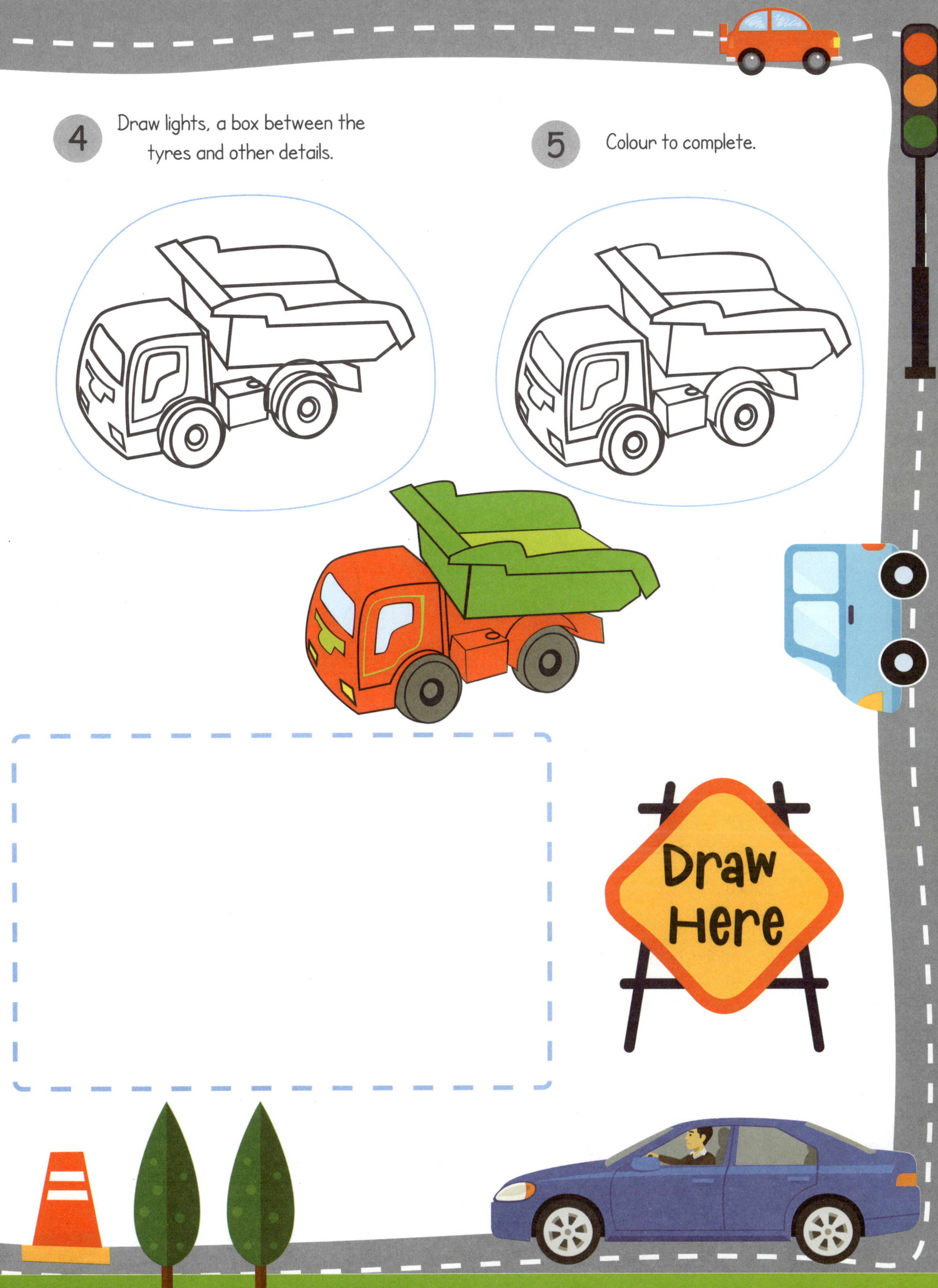

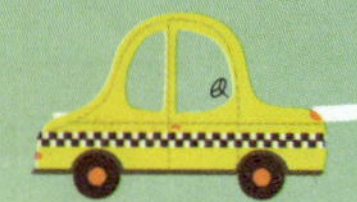

TRACTOR

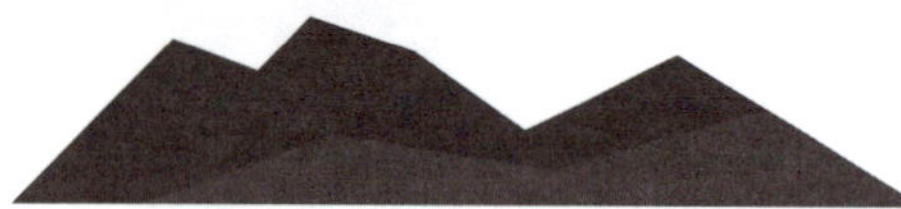

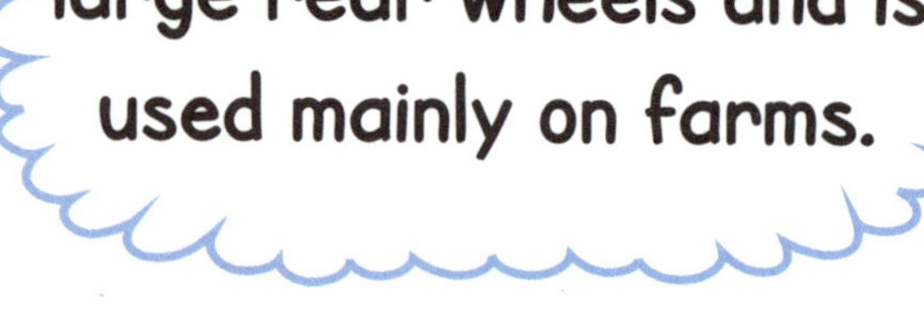

This is a tractor. It has large rear wheels and is used mainly on farms.

1 Draw one small, one half and one big circle for tyres. Draw lines for the body.

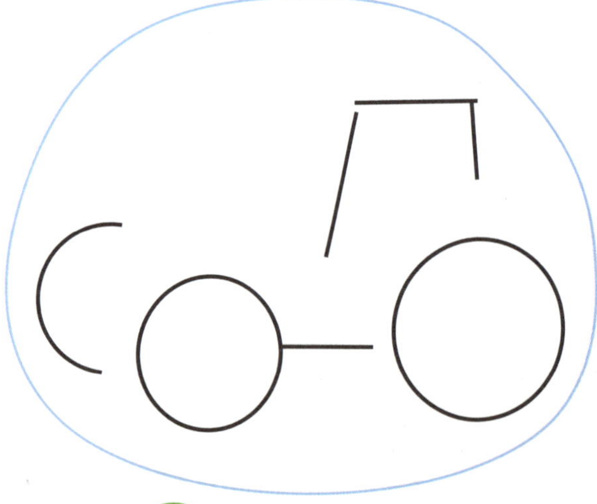

2 Outline the tyres. Draw lines and squares to make the body and mudflaps.

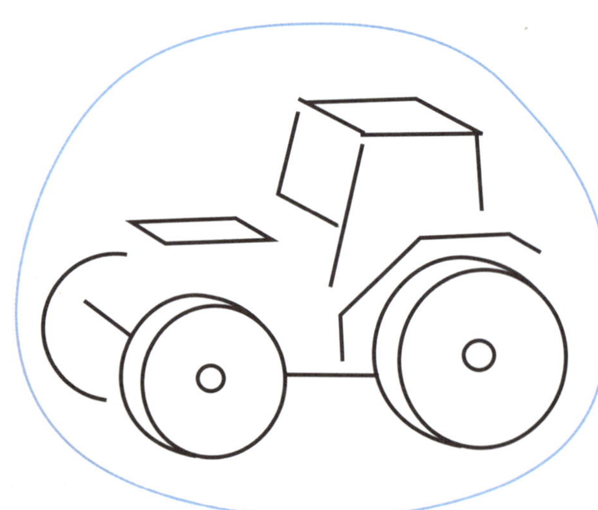

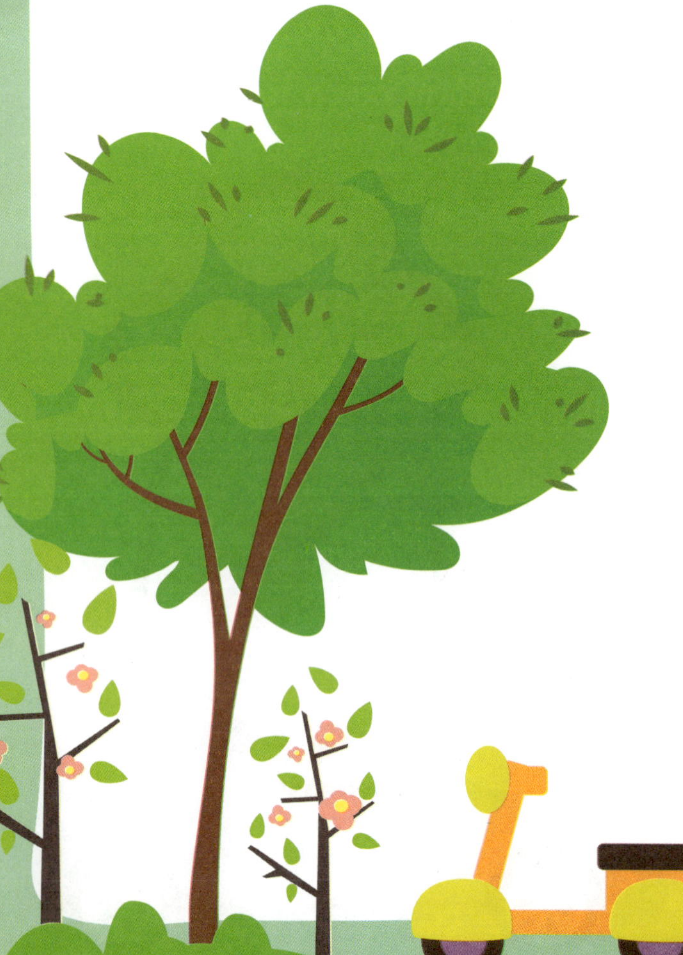

3 Draw the head light, lines and details to make the outer body. Draw the inner parts of the tyres.

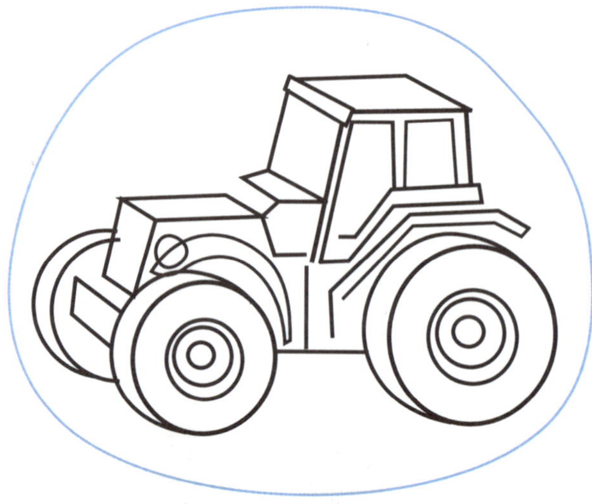

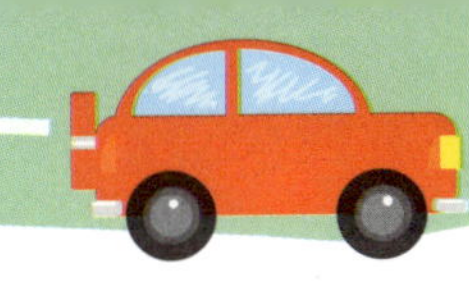

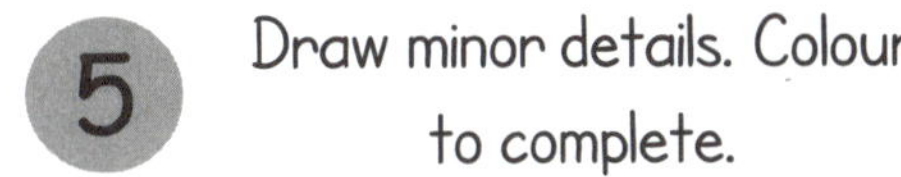

4 Draw the inside parts of the tractor. Draw designs on the tyres.

5 Draw minor details. Colour to complete.

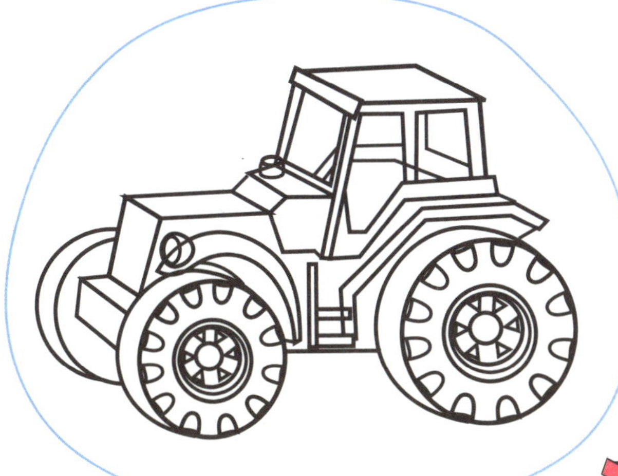

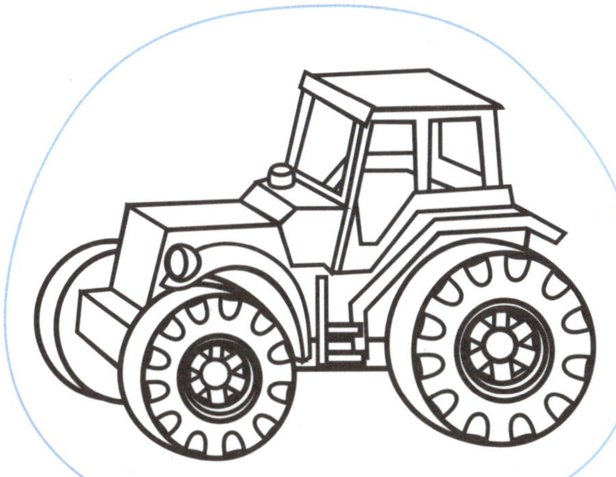

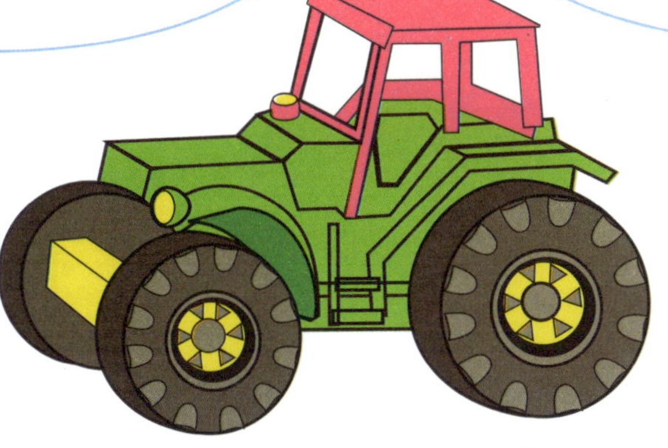

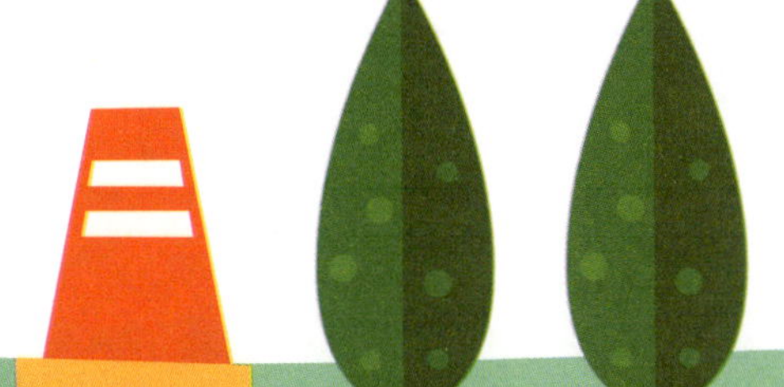

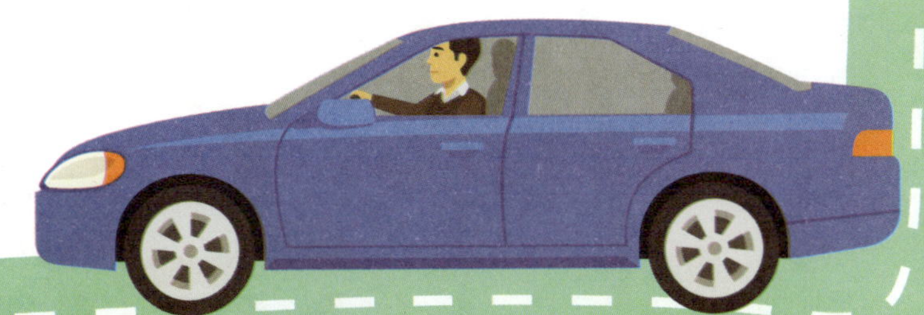

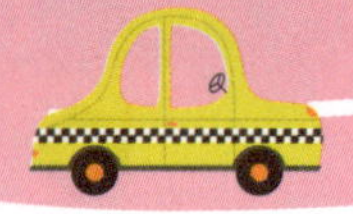

ROCKET

A rocket is a powerful machine soaring into space, carrying things beyond Earth's atmosphere.

1 Start by drawing a tall oval with a flat base for the main body of the rocket.

2 At the bottom of the rocket, draw two or three triangle-shaped fins on each side.

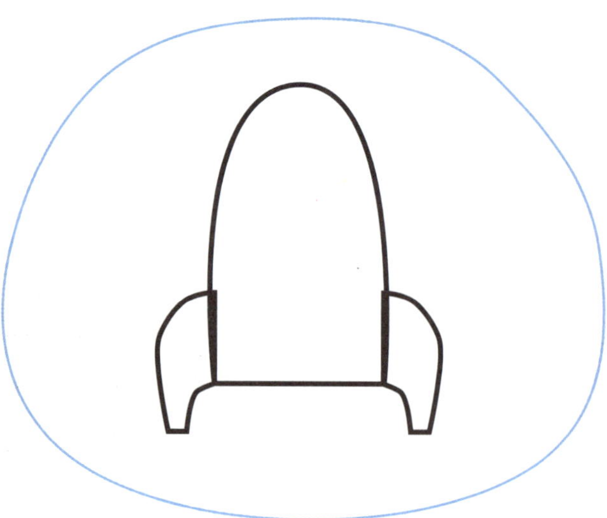

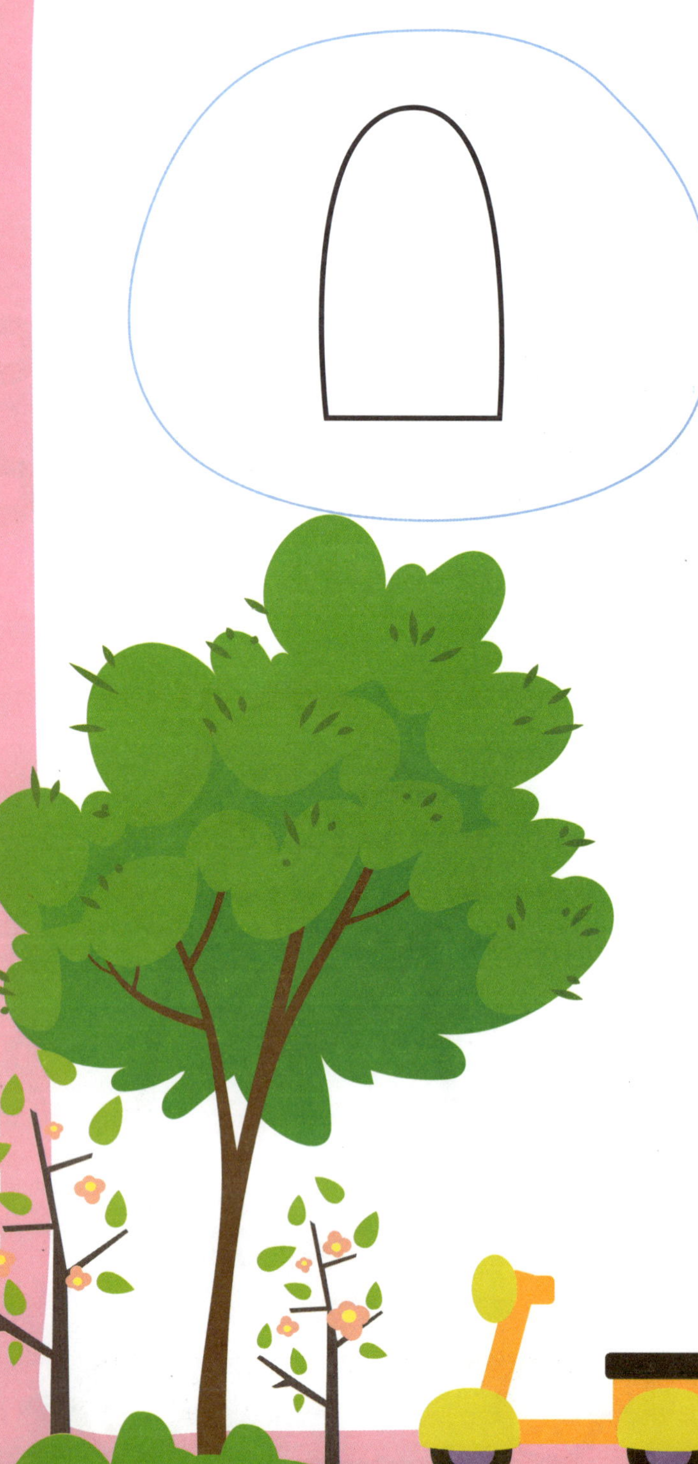

3 Add two circles near the top of the rocket to make the windows.

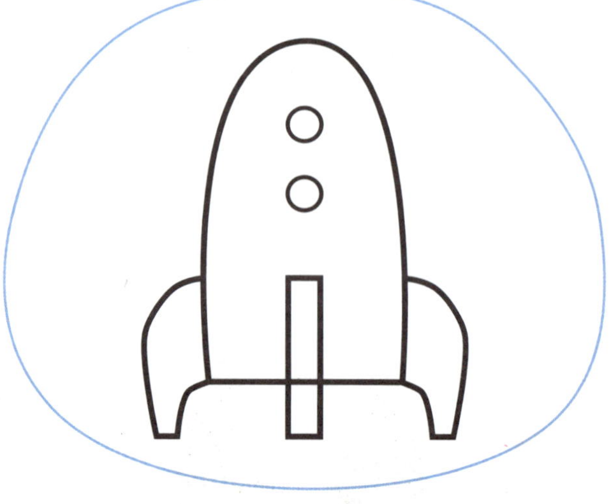

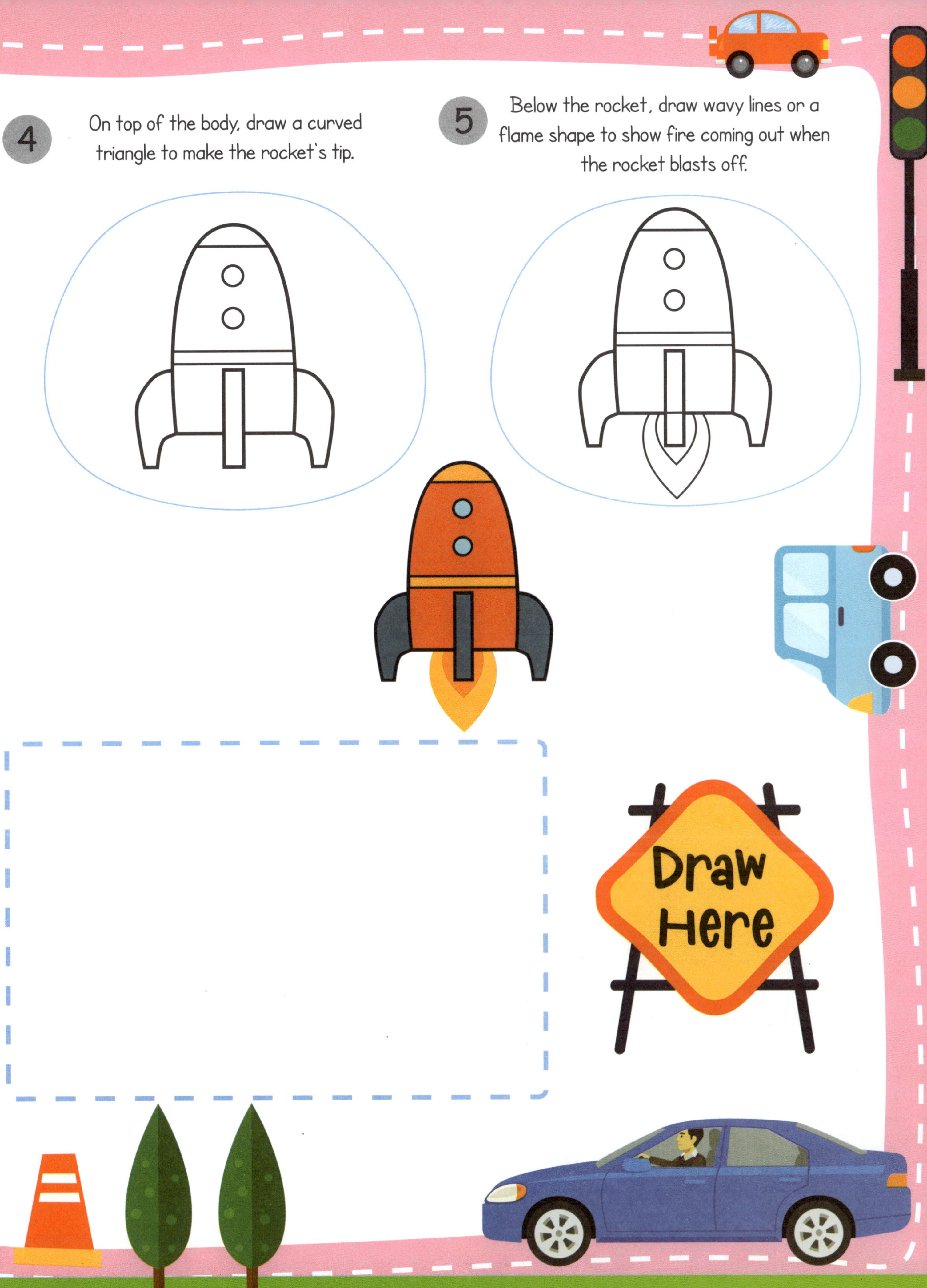
4
On top of the body, draw a curved triangle to make the rocket's tip.
5
Below the rocket, draw wavy lines or a flame shape to show fire coming out when the rocket blasts off.
Draw Here

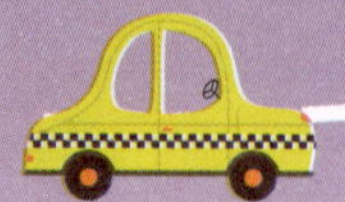

SHIP

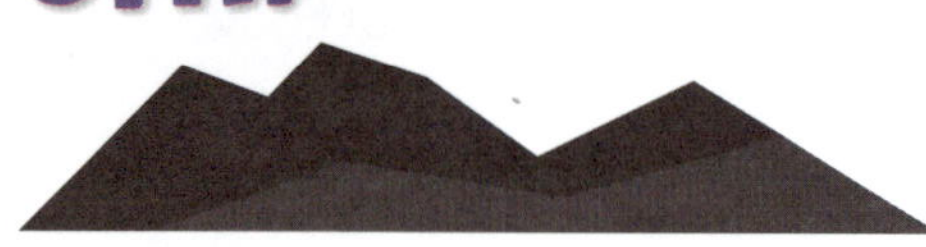

This is a ship. It's a large boat used for carrying passengers or cargo by sea.

1 Draw a conical, tilted leaf shape for the body. At the bottom, draw a straight line and join it above with a slight curve.

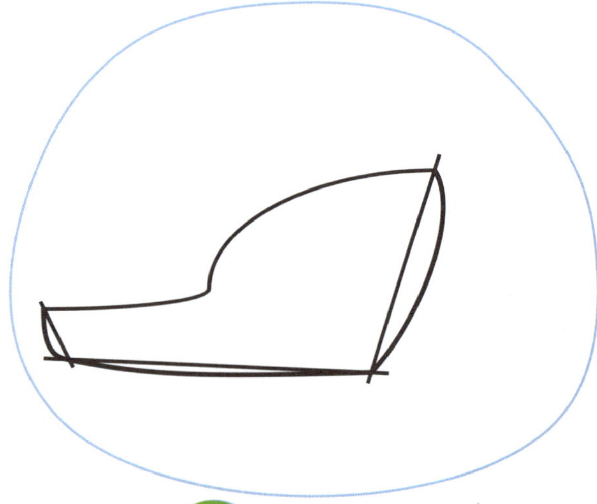

2 Above the leaf-shaped curve, draw a square with curved corners. Behind, draw a curve for the deck.

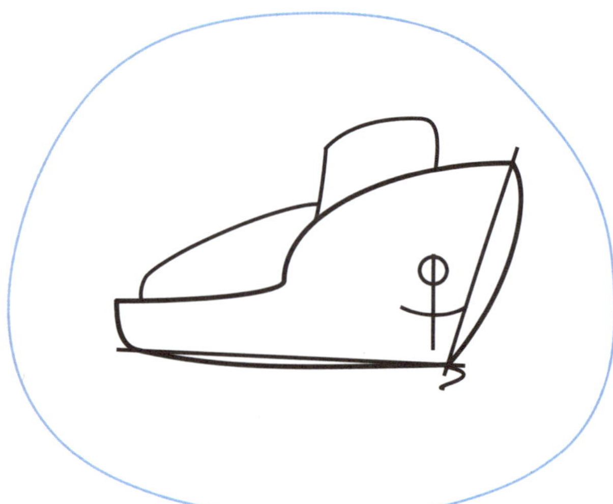

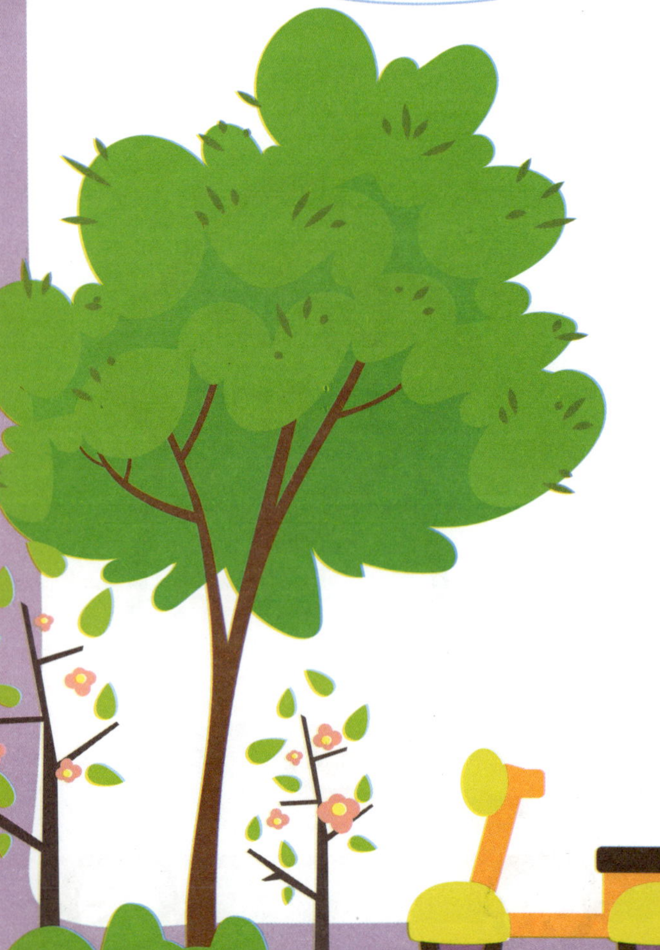

3 Draw the anchor, water ripples, window, cloud and deck outlines.

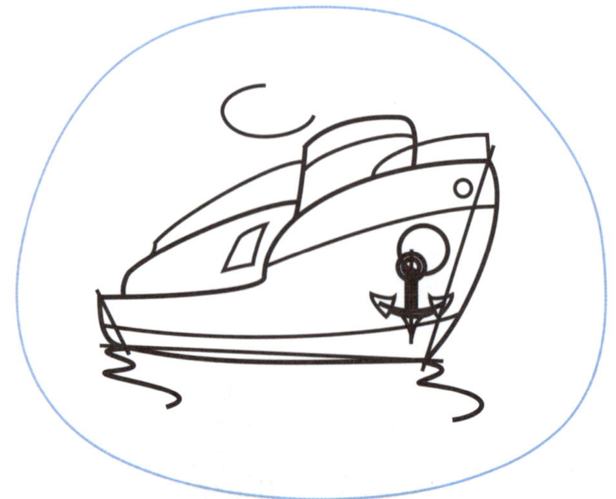

4 Complete the water ripples and clouds, draw more windows and draw circles on the ship front.

5 Draw straight lines on the ship's railing. Draw birds. Colour to complete.

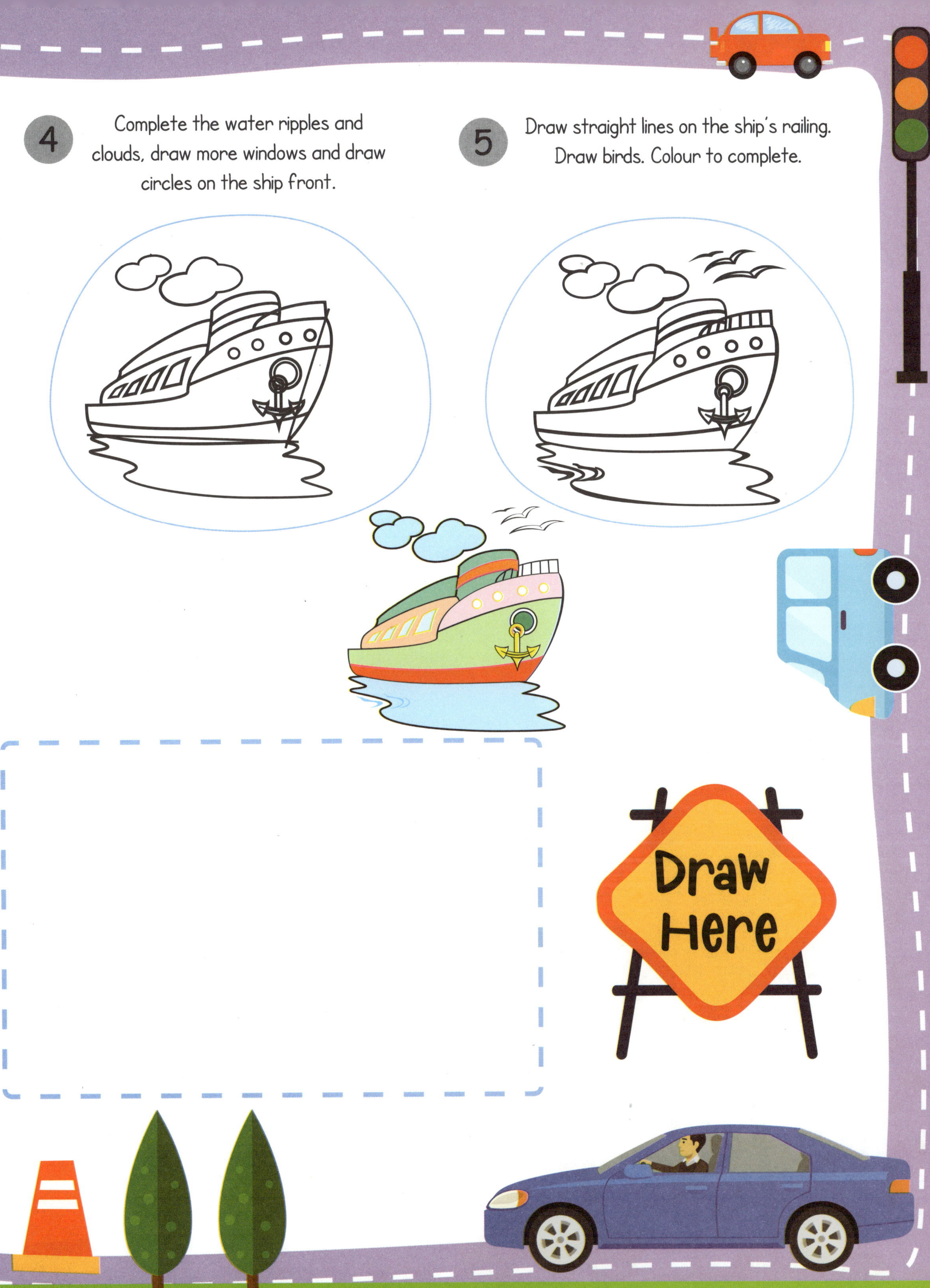

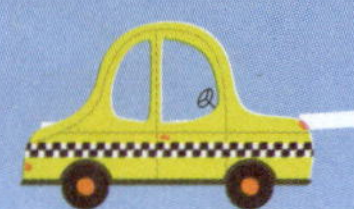

HELICOPTER

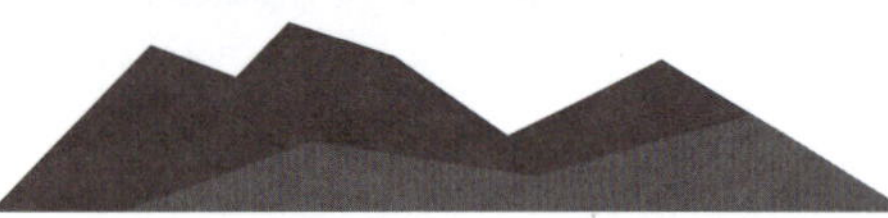

This is a helicopter. It's an aircraft that uses rotating wings called blades to fly.

1 Draw an oval shape and below it another for the body. Join two ovals with two perpendicular lines. Draw the tail.

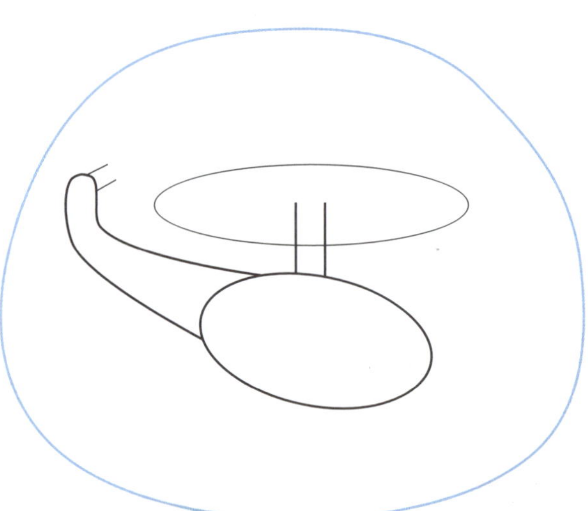

2 On the top oval, draw lines for wings. On the body, make another oval. Draw a "C" for the door and lines for the stand.

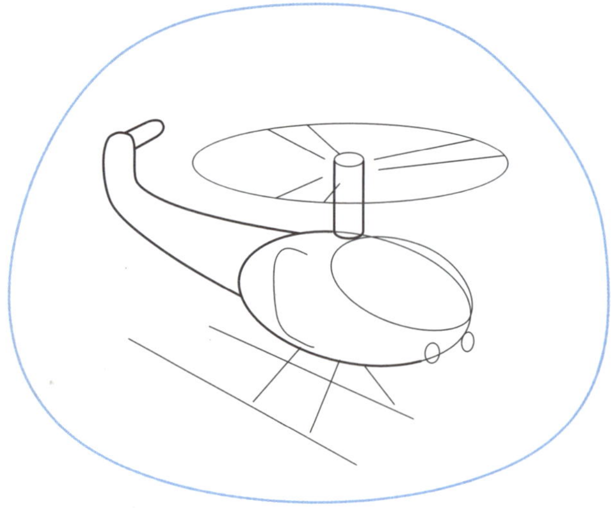

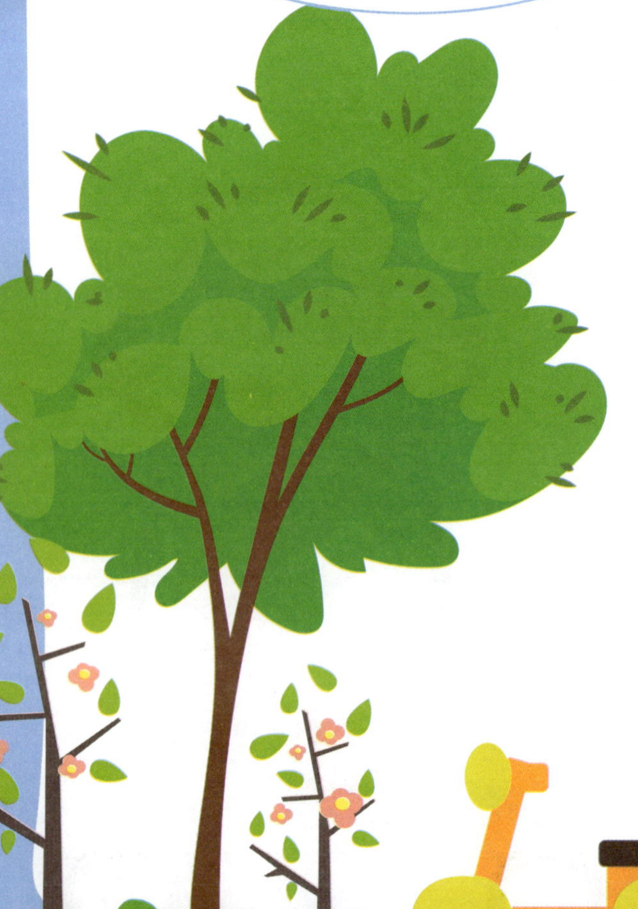

3 Draw the tail rotor, rotor mast, door and curved lines at the bottom to make landing skids.

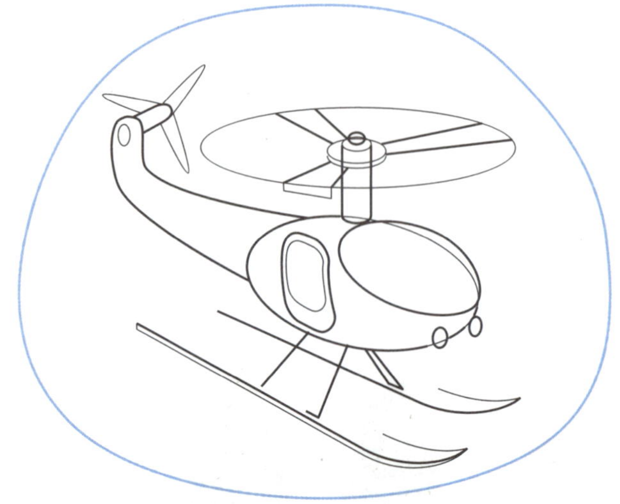

4 Complete the landing skids. Double the outlines. Draw lights.

5 Draw three curved lines on the tail. Erase any unwanted lines. Colour to complete.

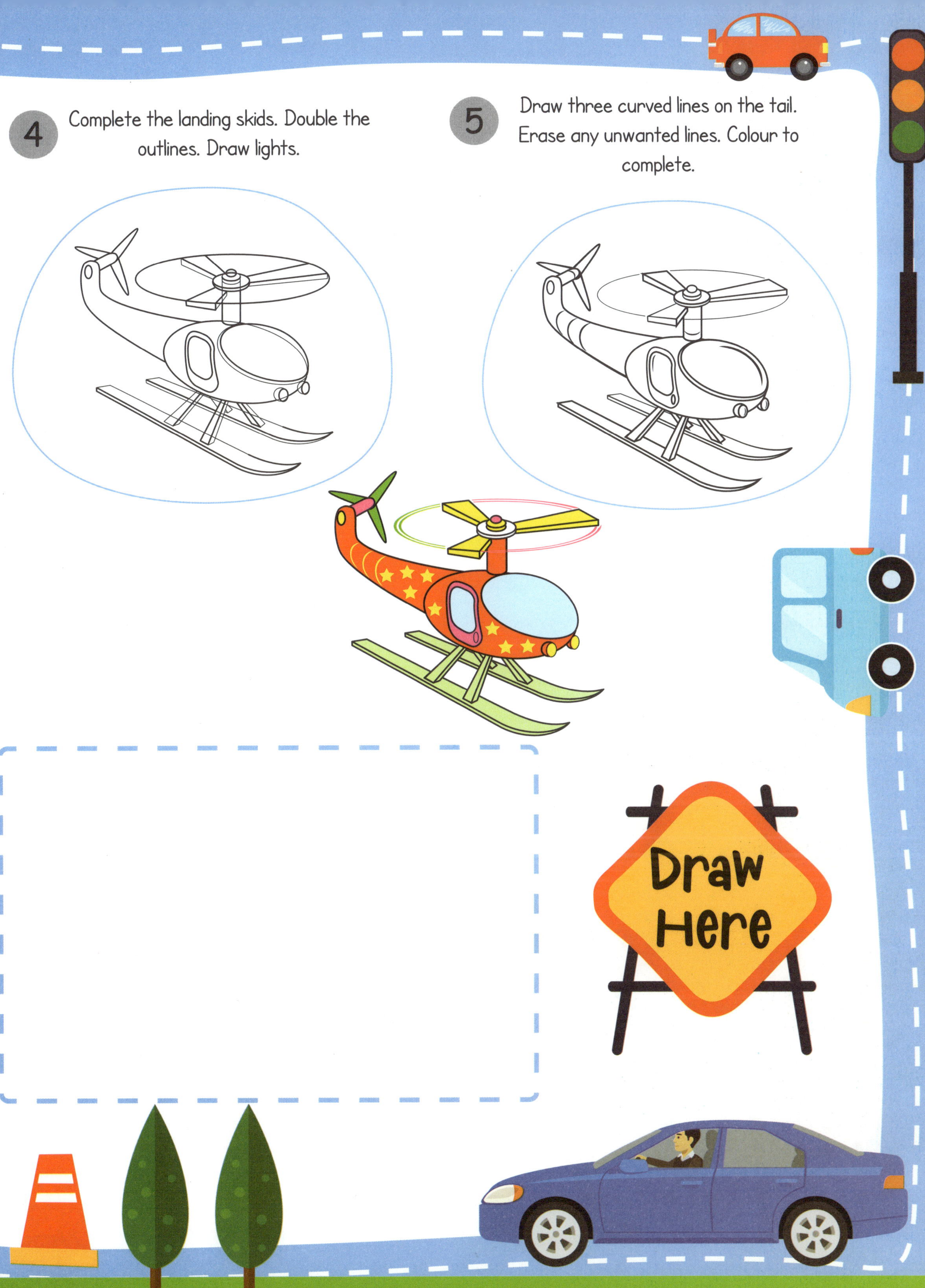

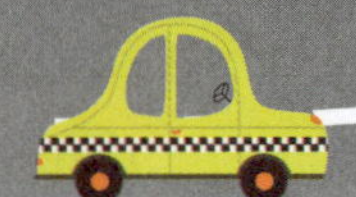

BOAT

This is a boat. It's a small vehicle used for travelling across water.

1 Draw a flat conical shape joined with a straight line at the back. From the center, draw a straight line and a curve for the sail.

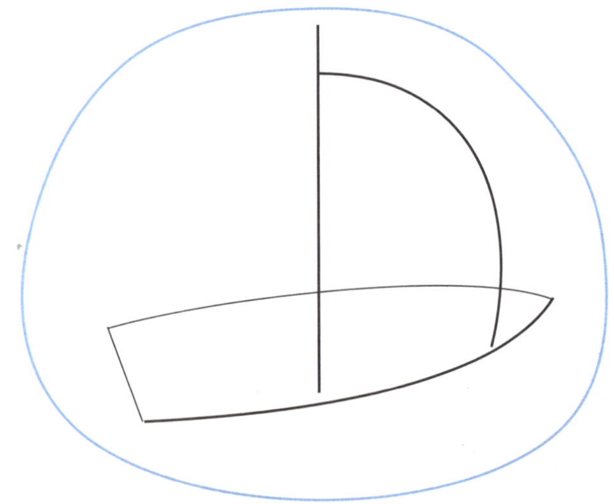

2 Double-line the straight line and draw a curve for the sail and base of the boat.

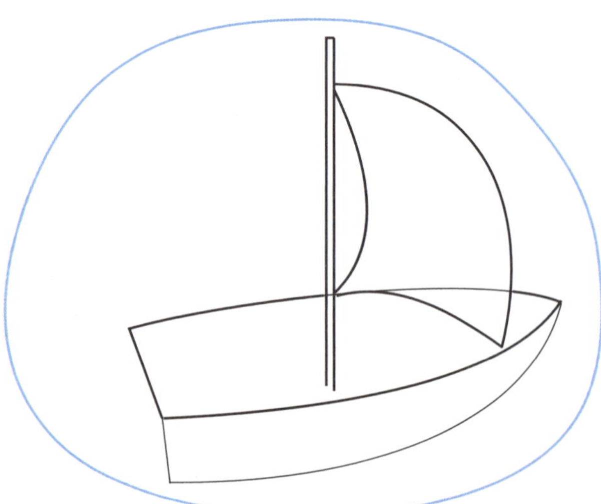

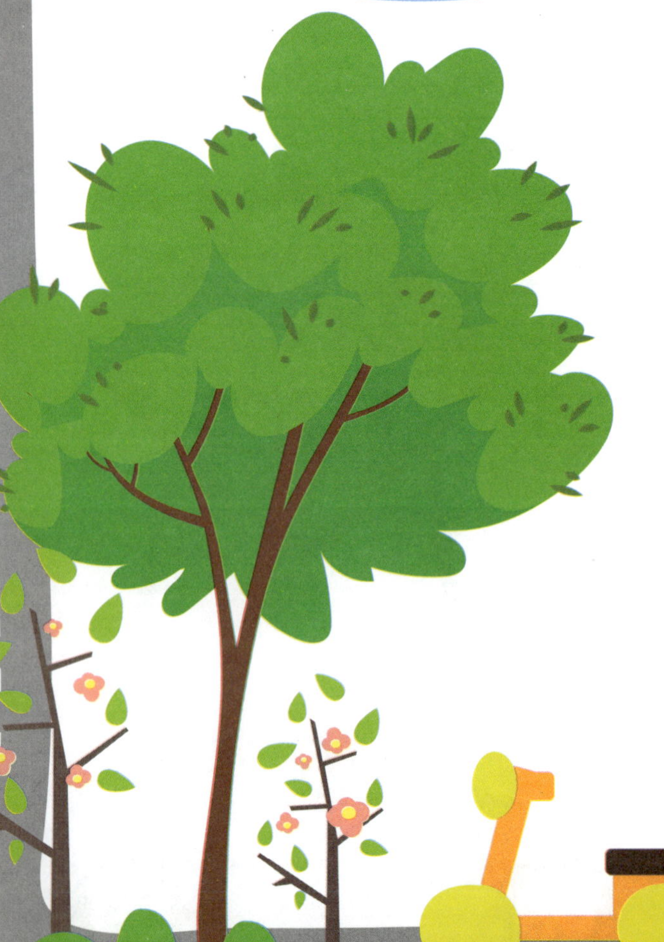

3 Draw a half rectangle on the left side for seating space. Draw a double outline for the boat.

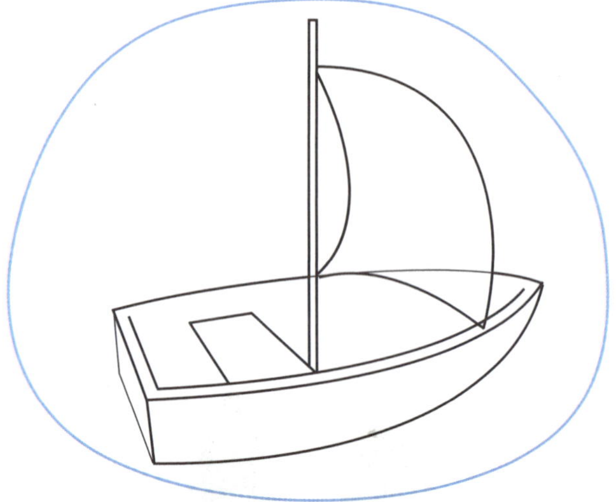

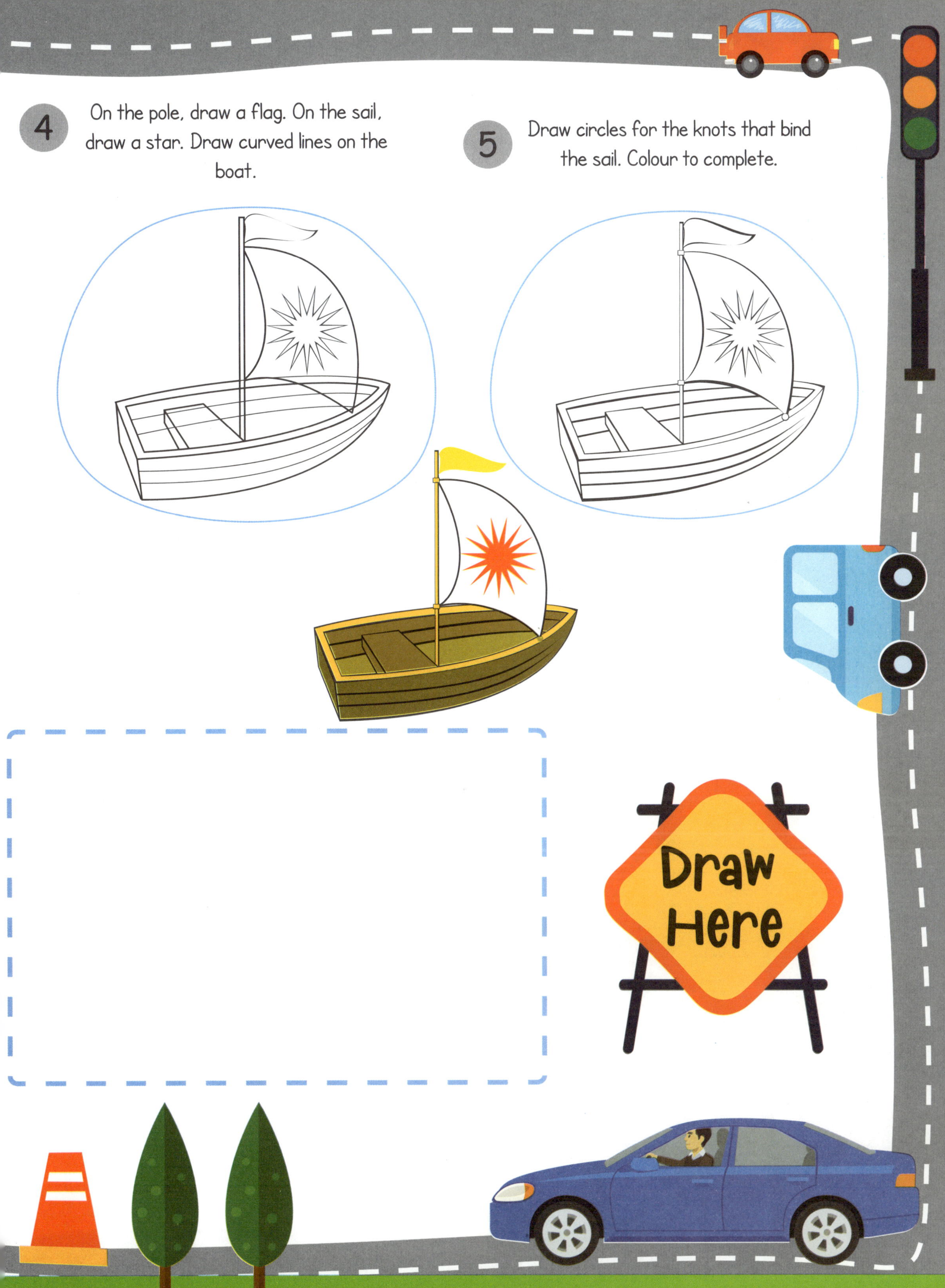

4
On the pole, draw a flag. On the sail, draw a star. Draw curved lines on the boat.
5
Draw circles for the knots that bind the sail. Colour to complete.
Draw Here

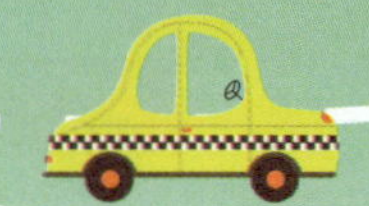

BIKE

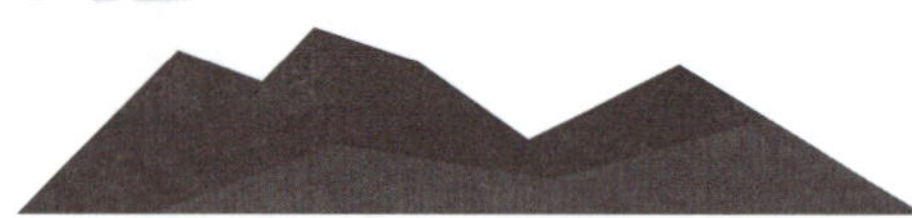

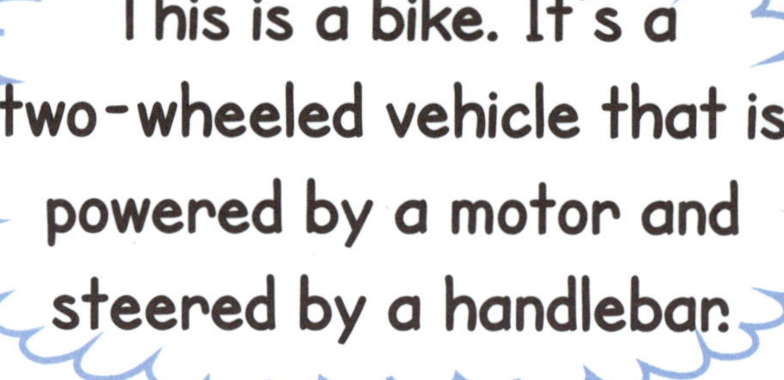

This is a bike. It's a two-wheeled vehicle that is powered by a motor and steered by a handlebar.

1 Draw an egg shape in the center and two circles on its either side. Inside those circles, towards the left, draw one circle each.

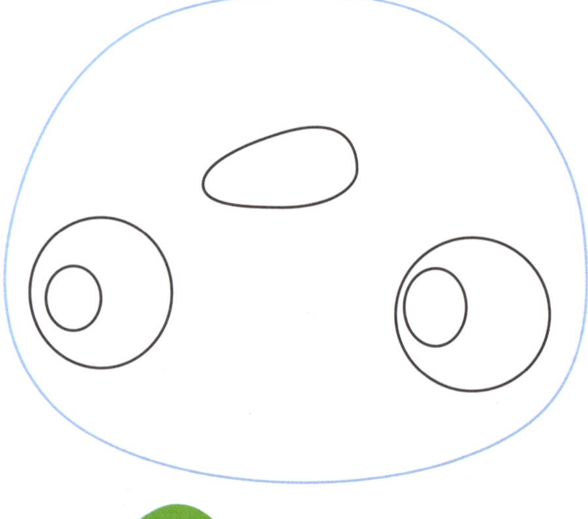

2 Behind the egg shape, draw the seat. Draw the handle, the bike's front body and outline all the parts.

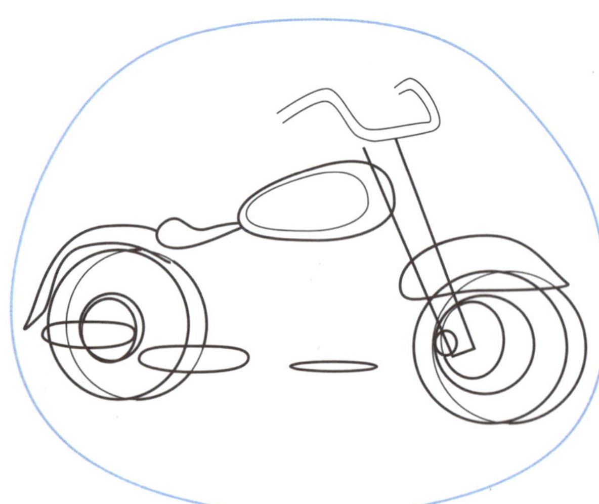

3 Draw a circle below the egg shape. Draw details on the handles and body. Draw head lights, an oil cap and mudguards.

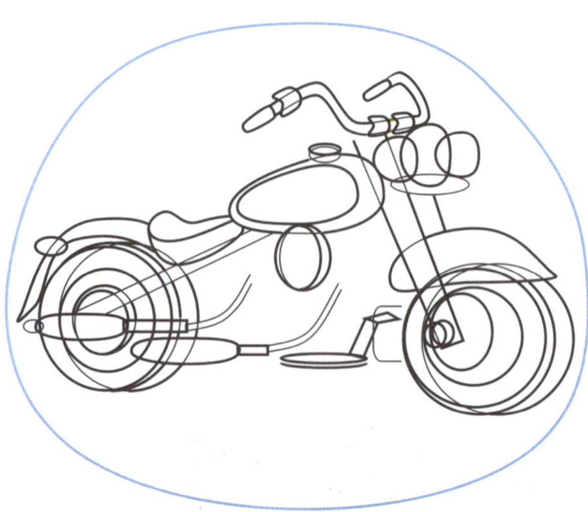

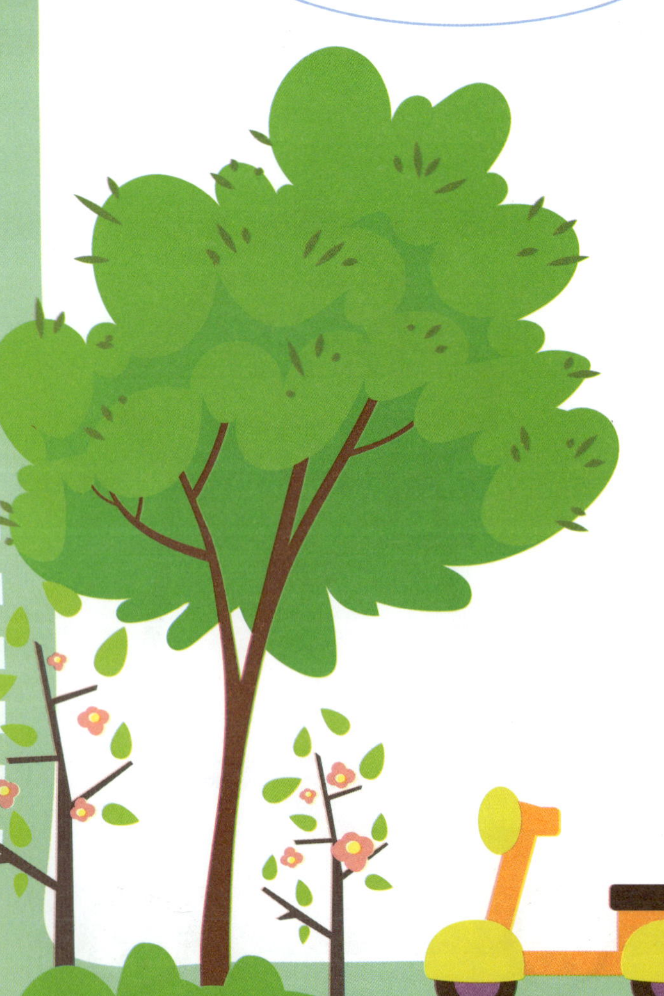

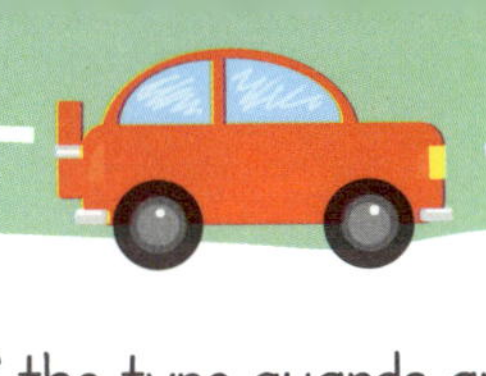

4 Draw the coil on both sides of the circle. Draw mirrors, a footrest and minor details.

5 Darken the outline of the tyre guards and the fuel tank. Erase unwanted lines. Colour to complete.

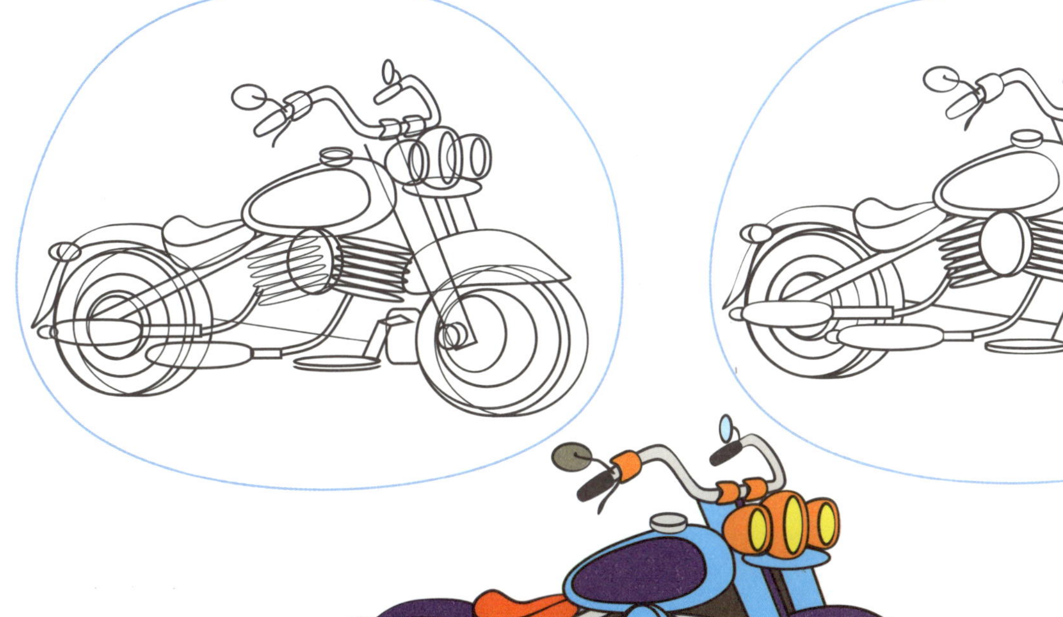

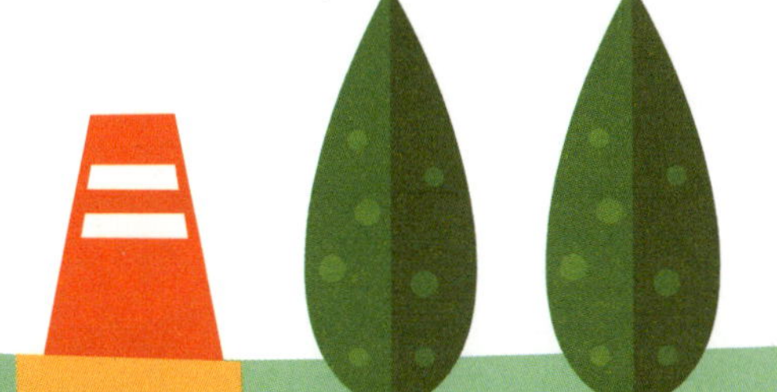

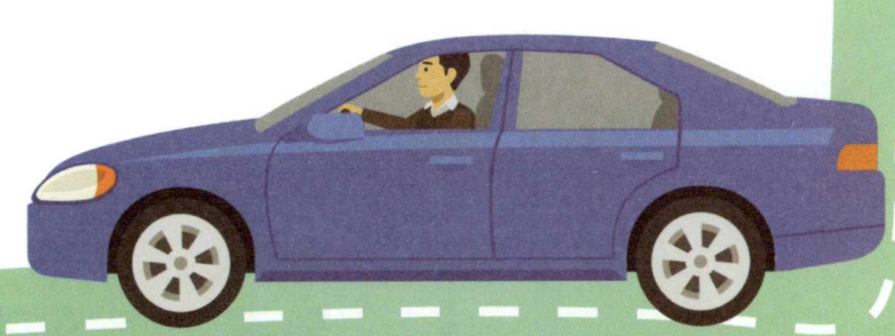

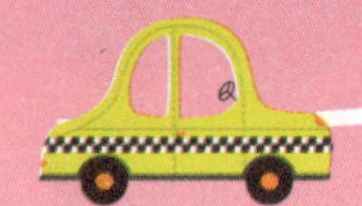

AMBULANCE

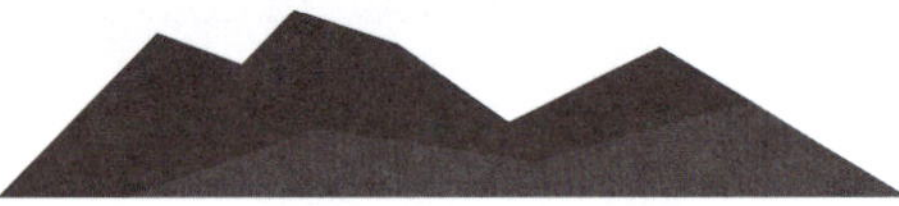

This is an ambulance. It's used to transport sick and injured people to the hospital.

1 Draw two circles for wheels. Draw the shape of the vehicle's body over the wheels.

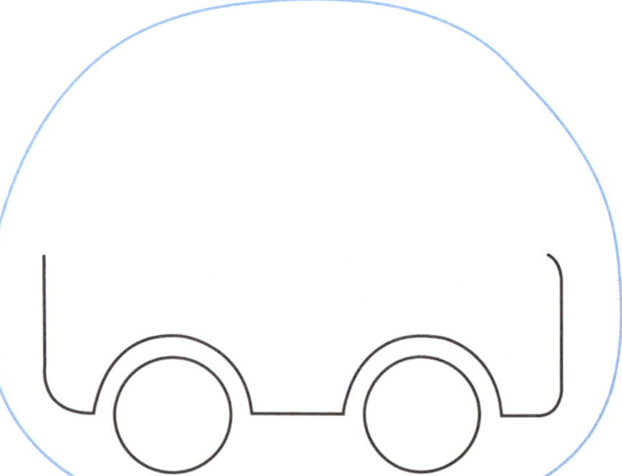

2 Stretch lines to complete the outer shape of the vehicle.

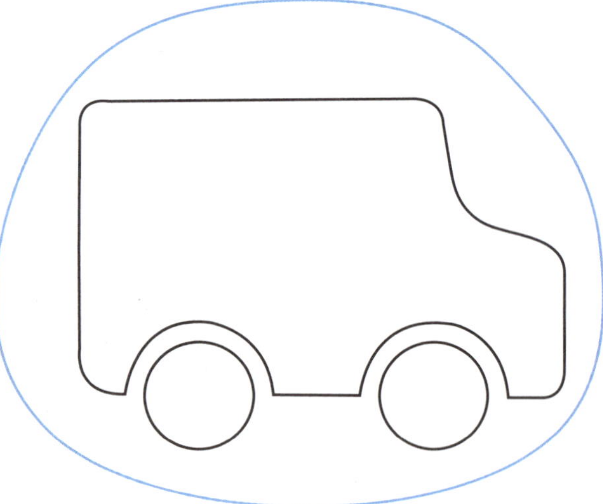

3 Draw two squares, one big and one small, for the windows.

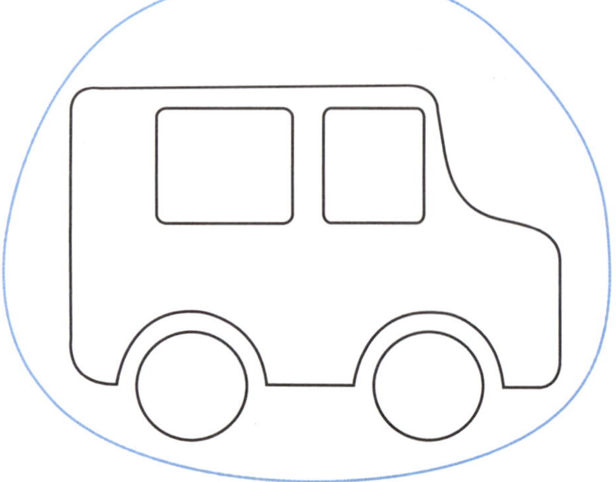

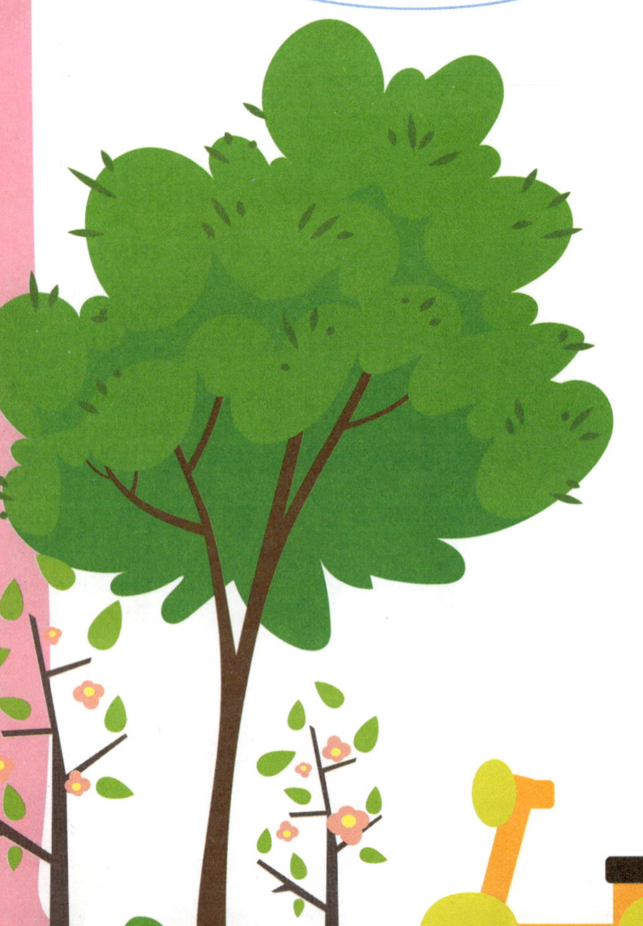

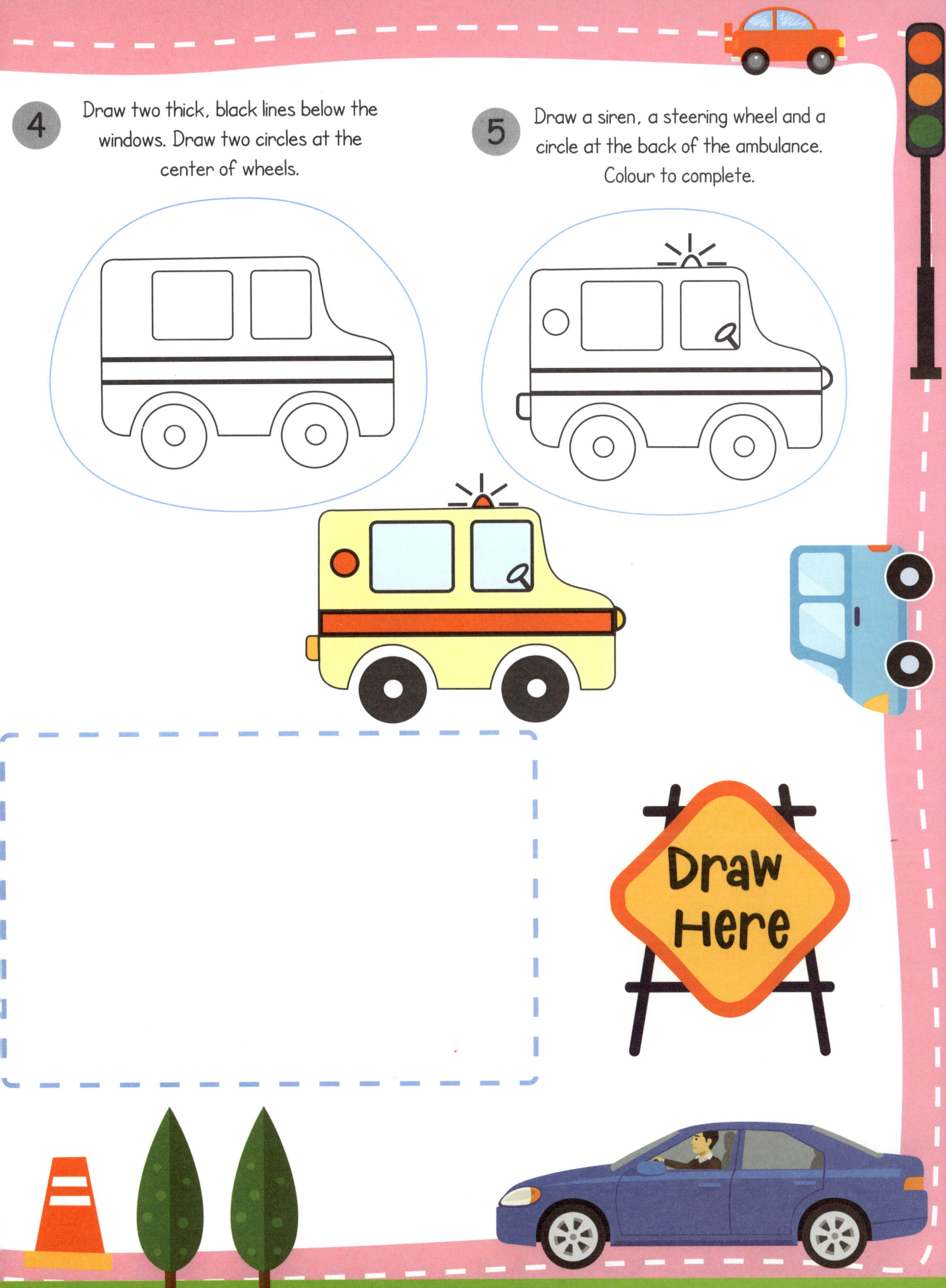
4
Draw two thick, black lines below the windows. Draw two circles at the center of wheels.
5
Draw a siren, a steering wheel and a circle at the back of the ambulance. Colour to complete.
Draw
Here

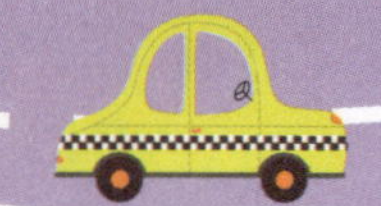

SUBMARINE

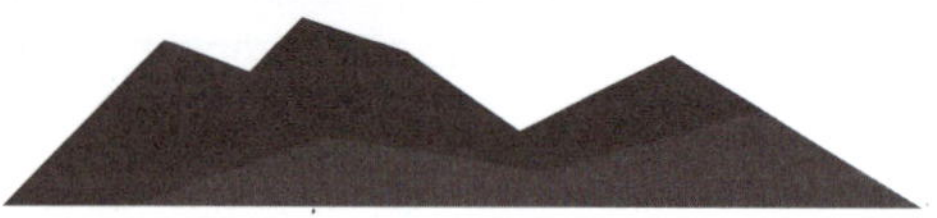

This is a submarine. It's a vessel that can go underwater.

1 Draw an oval shape.

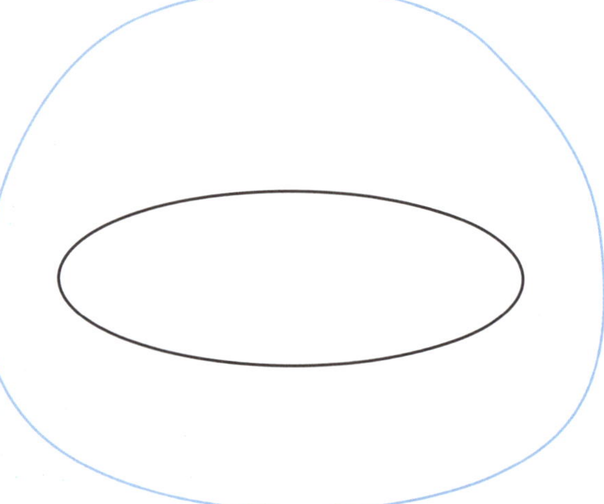

2 Draw three circles at equal distances inside the oval.

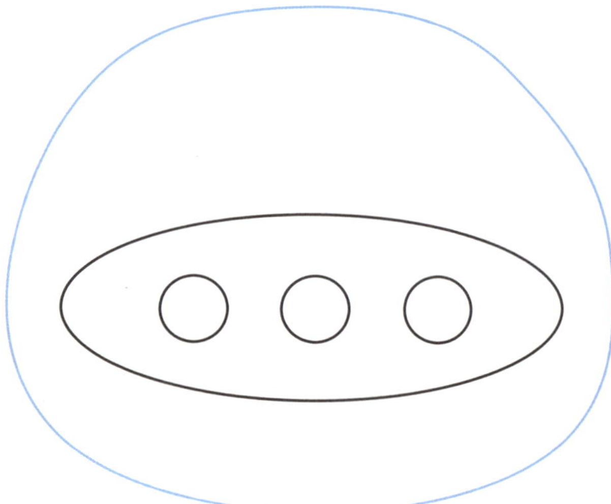

3 Draw two directional rudders at the end of the submarine. Draw a curve a the front part.

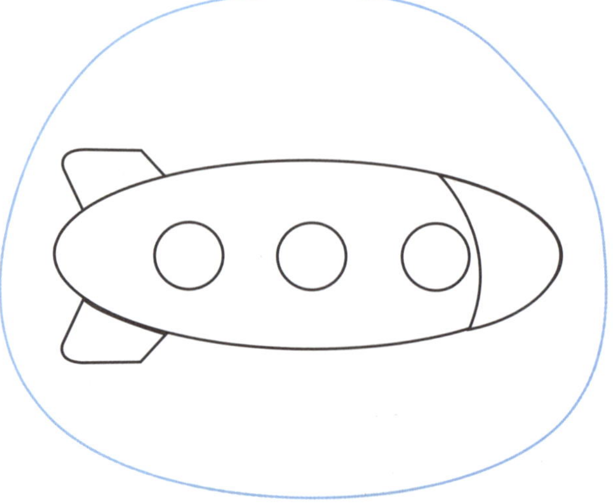

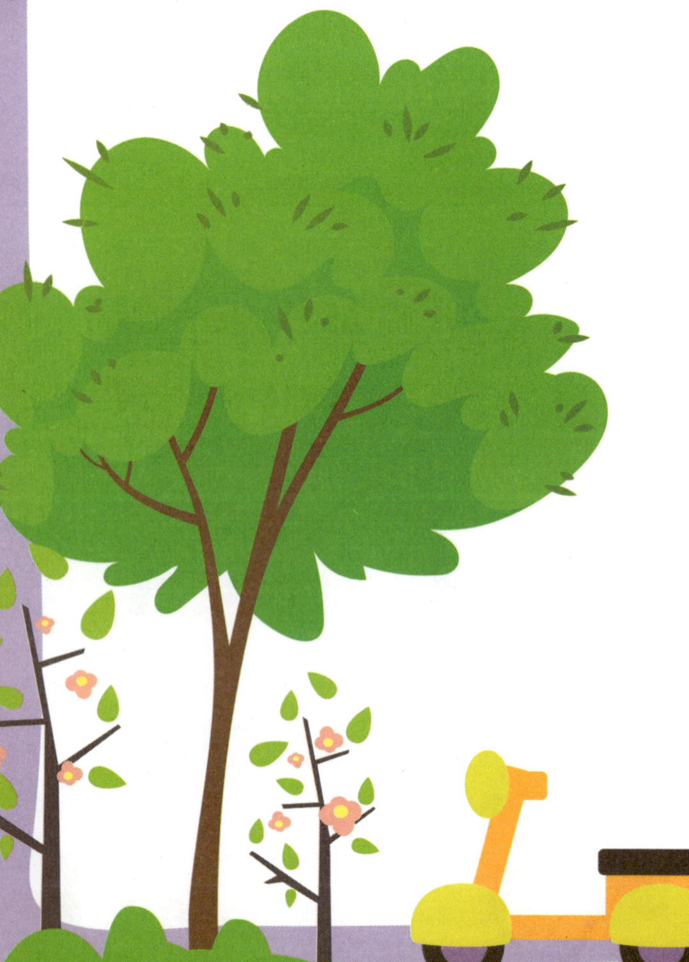

4 Draw oval-shaped propellers at the back. Draw a curved tower at the top.

5 Draw a periscope at the top of the tower. Colour to complete.

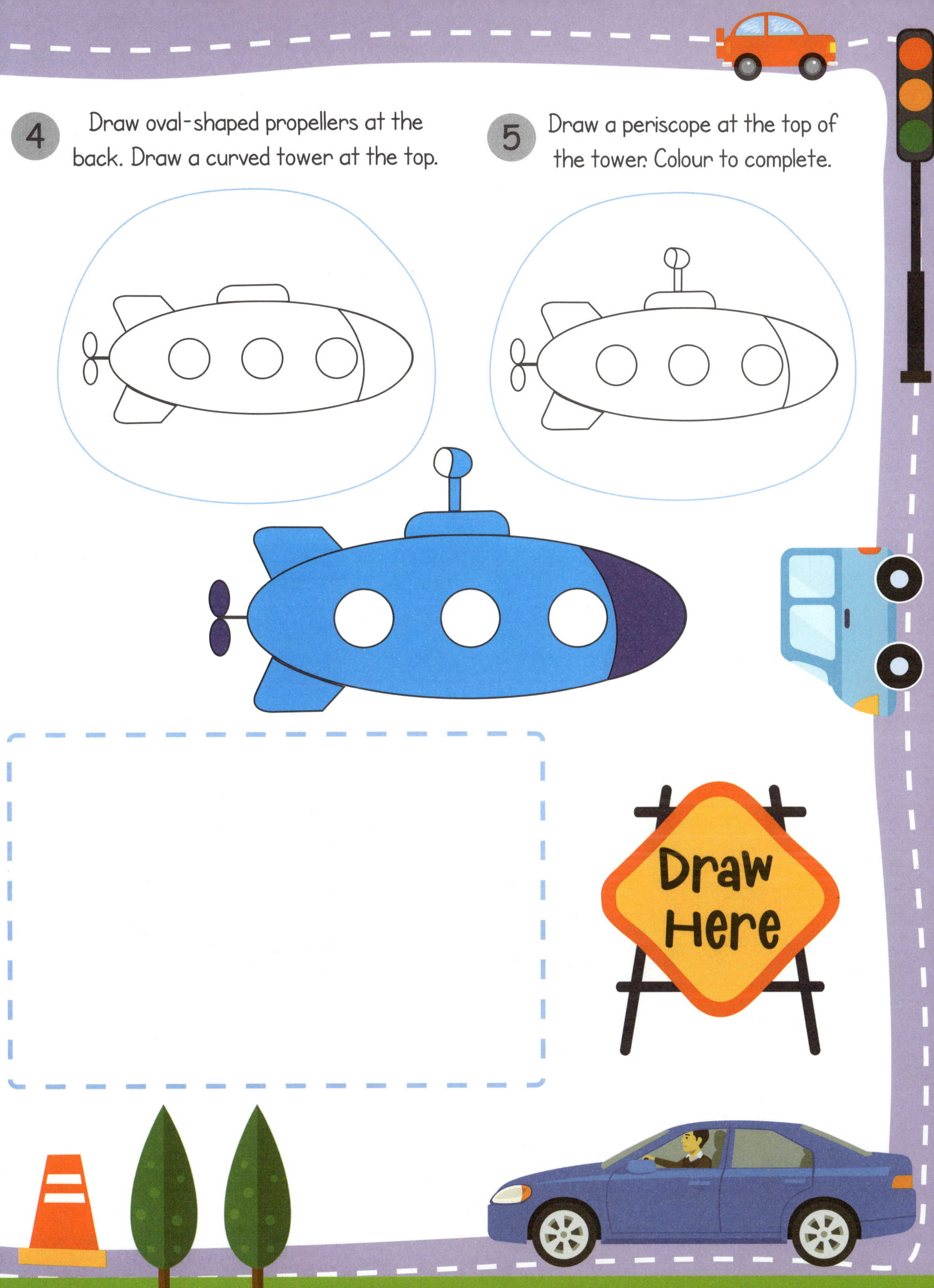

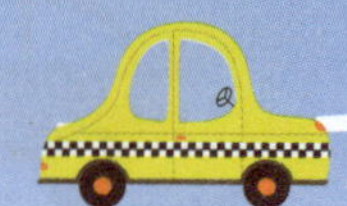

TANKER TRUCK

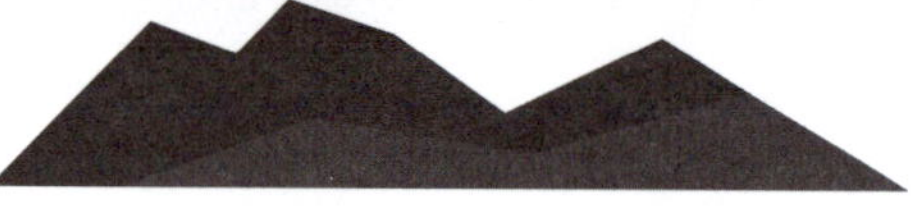

This is a tanker truck. It has a tank-like body suitable for transporting gases and liquids.

1 Draw a small rectangle and on its right side, draw a bigger rectangle and curve it from the corners.

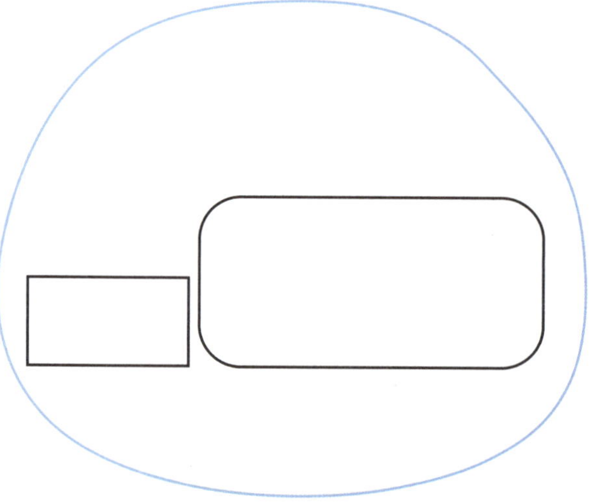

2 Draw a border line with curved ends under both rectangles. Draw a shape for the front body.

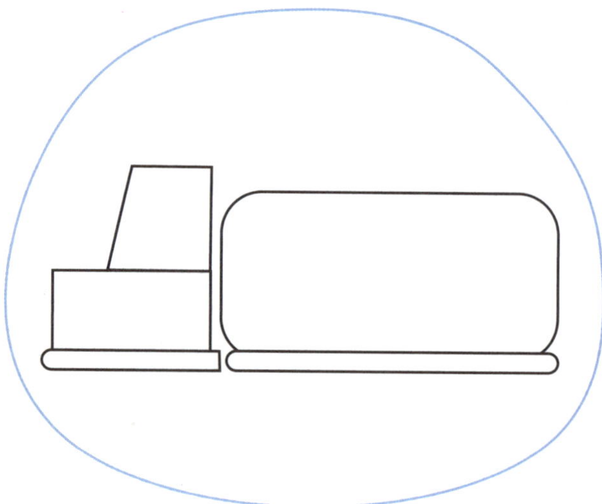

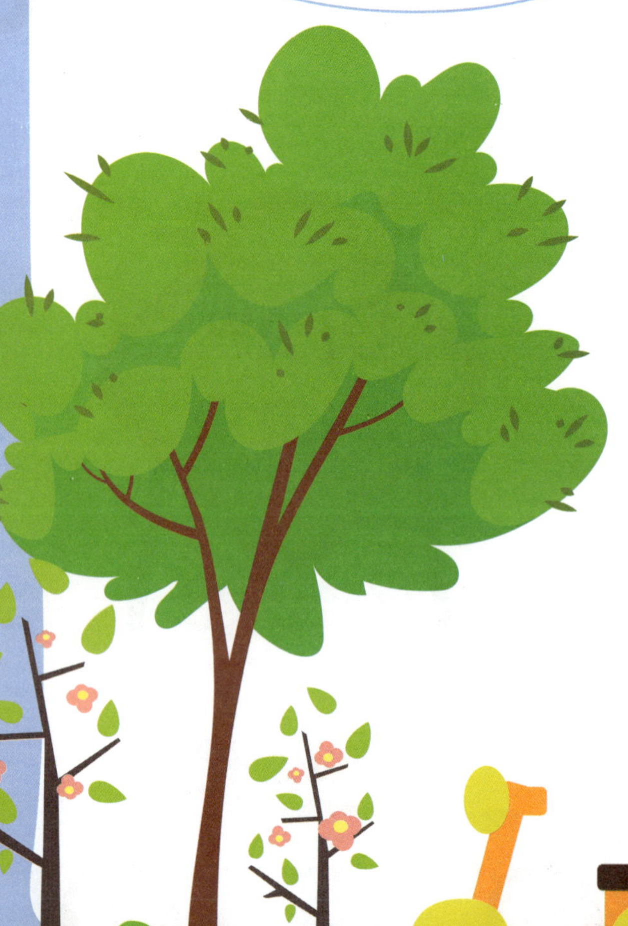

3 Double the outline of the front body. Draw circles for wheels. Draw details.

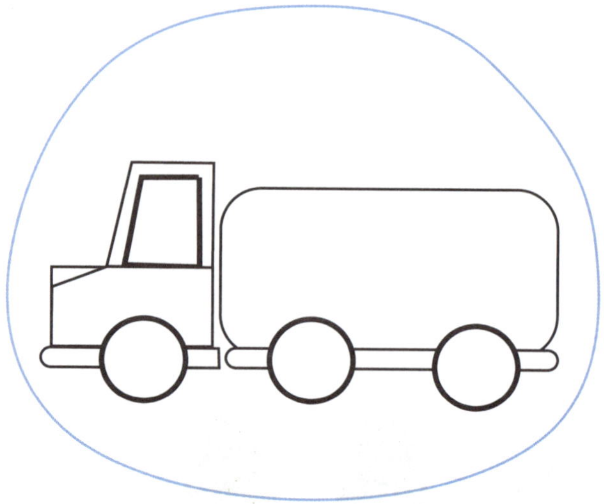

4 Draw curved lines on the back body. Outline wheels. Add details.

5 Draw the light, the upper part of the tanker and other details. Colour to complete.

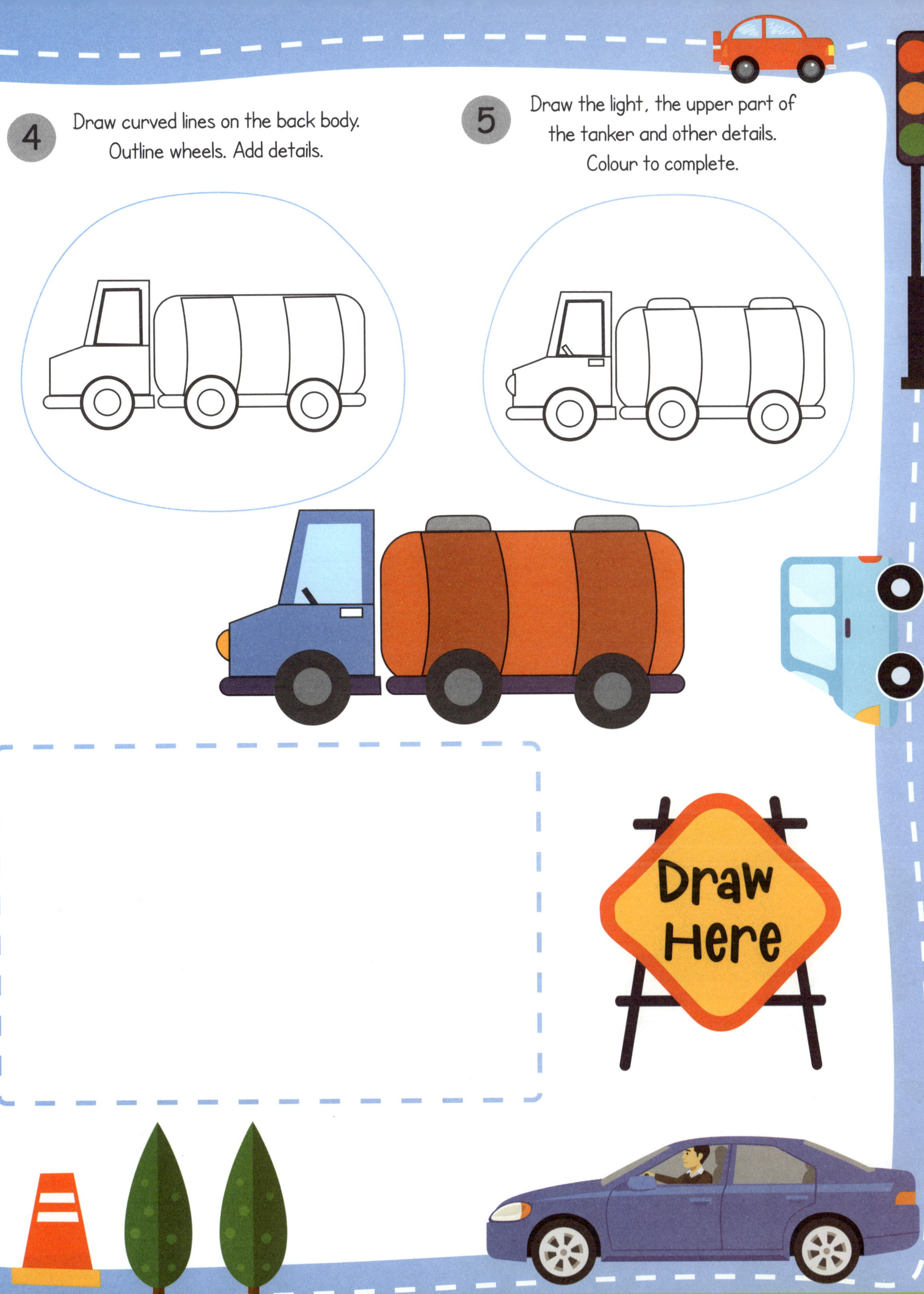

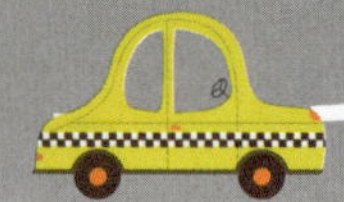

TAXI

This is a taxi. It's a car for hire with a driver.

1 Draw a rectangle and over it, draw a triangle with its right side curved.

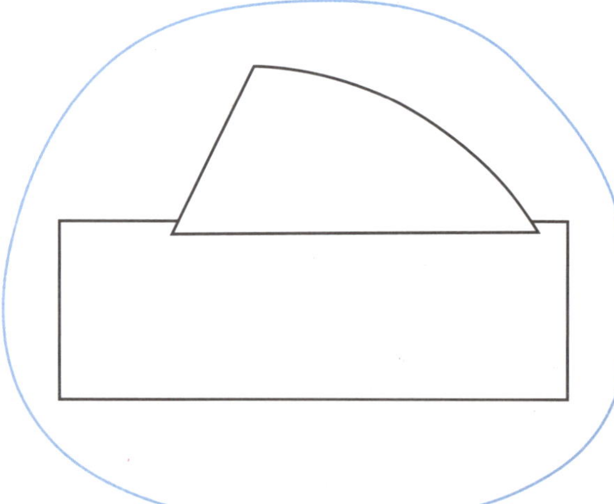

2 Draw a curve on the front and a circle for light. Draw an outline at the bottom.

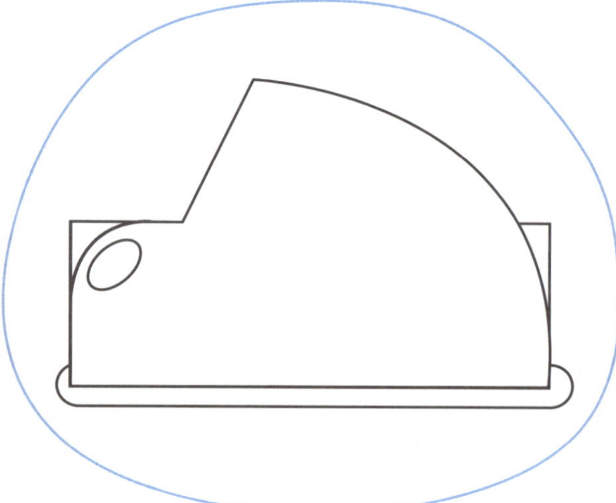

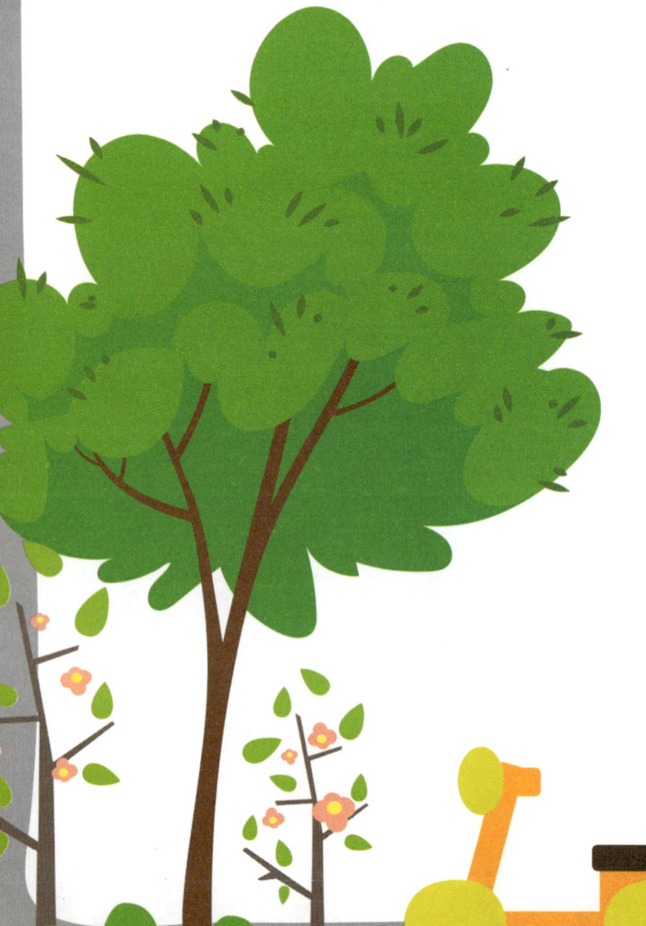

3 Draw the car's window and its outline. Also draw its tyres and a box at the top of the triangle for its taxi sign.

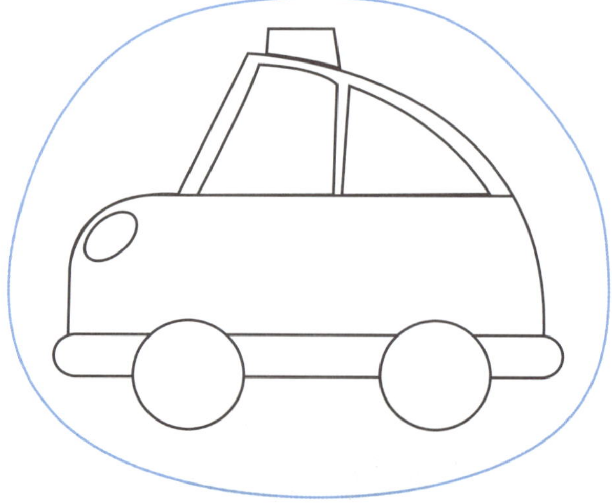

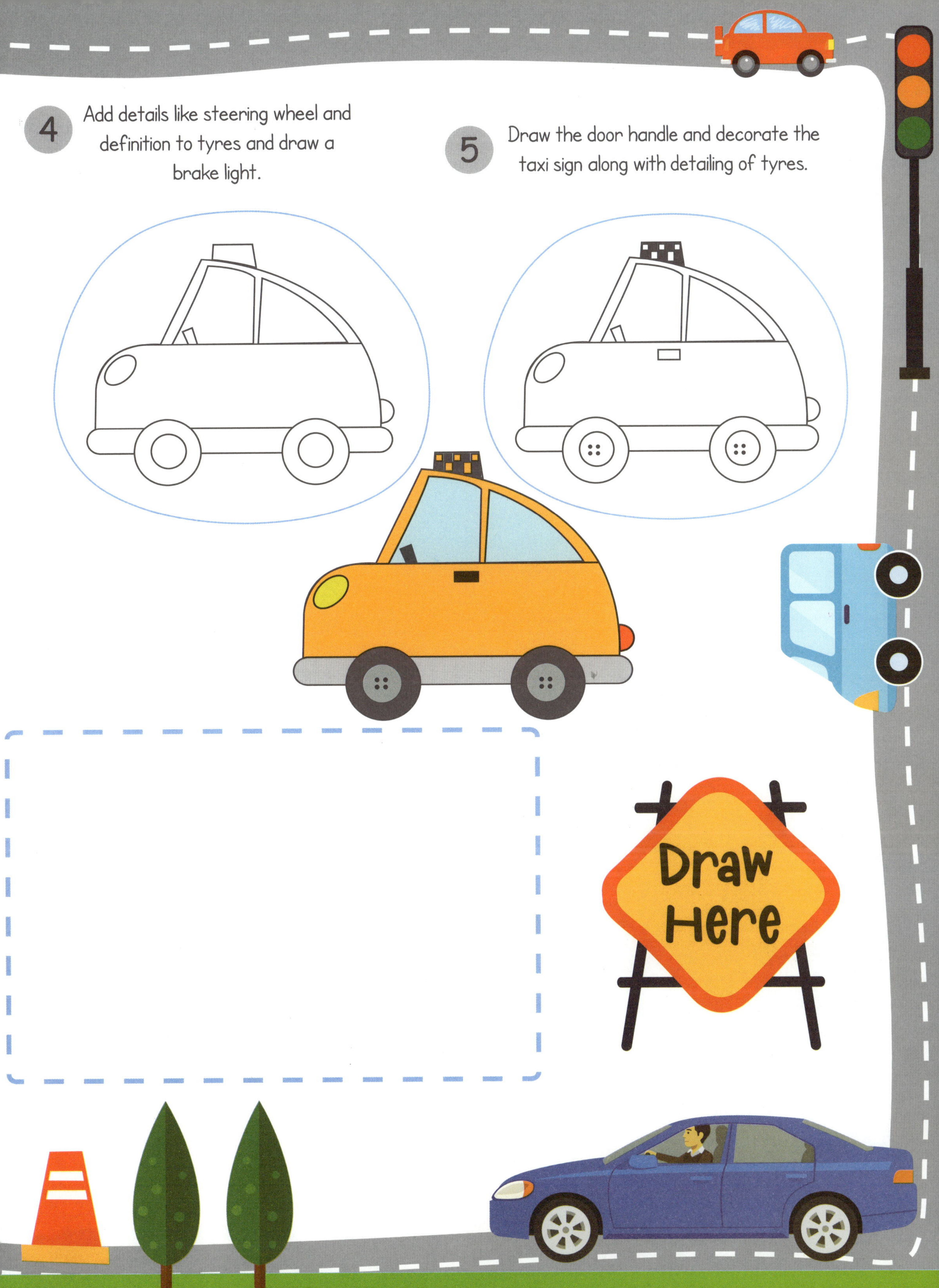
4
Add details like steering wheel and definition to tyres and draw a brake light.
5
Draw the door handle and decorate the taxi sign along with detailing of tyres.
Draw Here

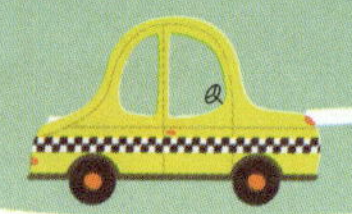

BIPLANE

This is a biplane. It's an aircraft with two pairs of wings, one above the other.

1 Draw an elongated oval shape with a circle in the front. Intersecting at the end, draw a wing for the biplane.

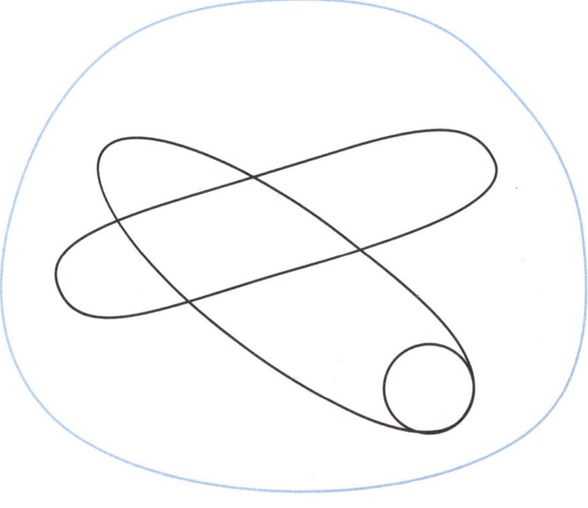

2 Draw a wing on the lower side with a fan on the circle. Draw the tail.

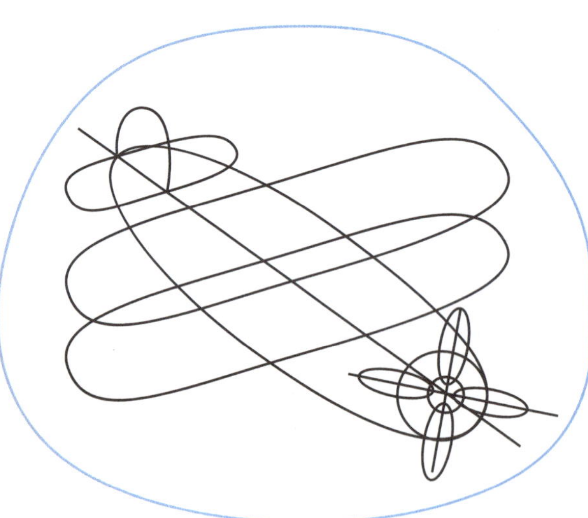

3 Draw the opening of the cockpit.

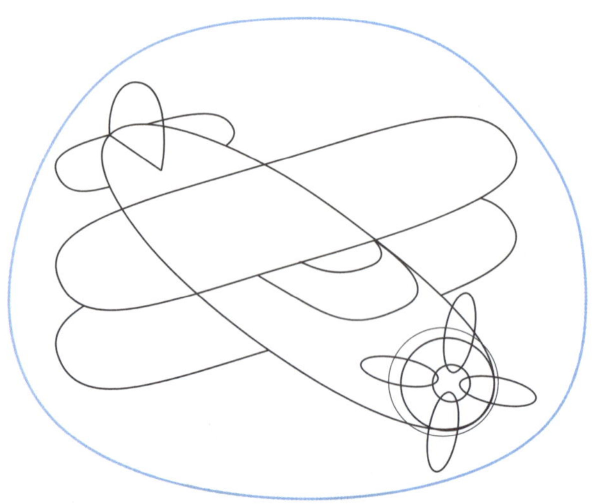

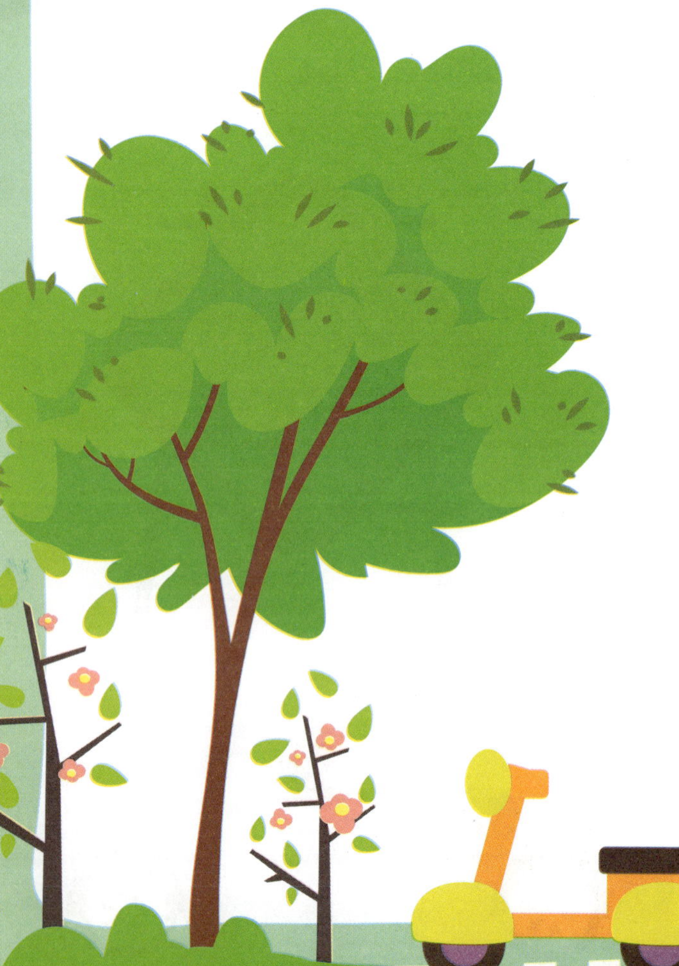

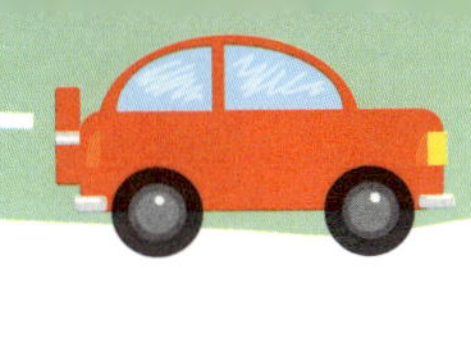

4 Double outline the wings with a dark pencil. Erase unwanted lines.

5 Draw the connectors between the two wings. Colour to complete.

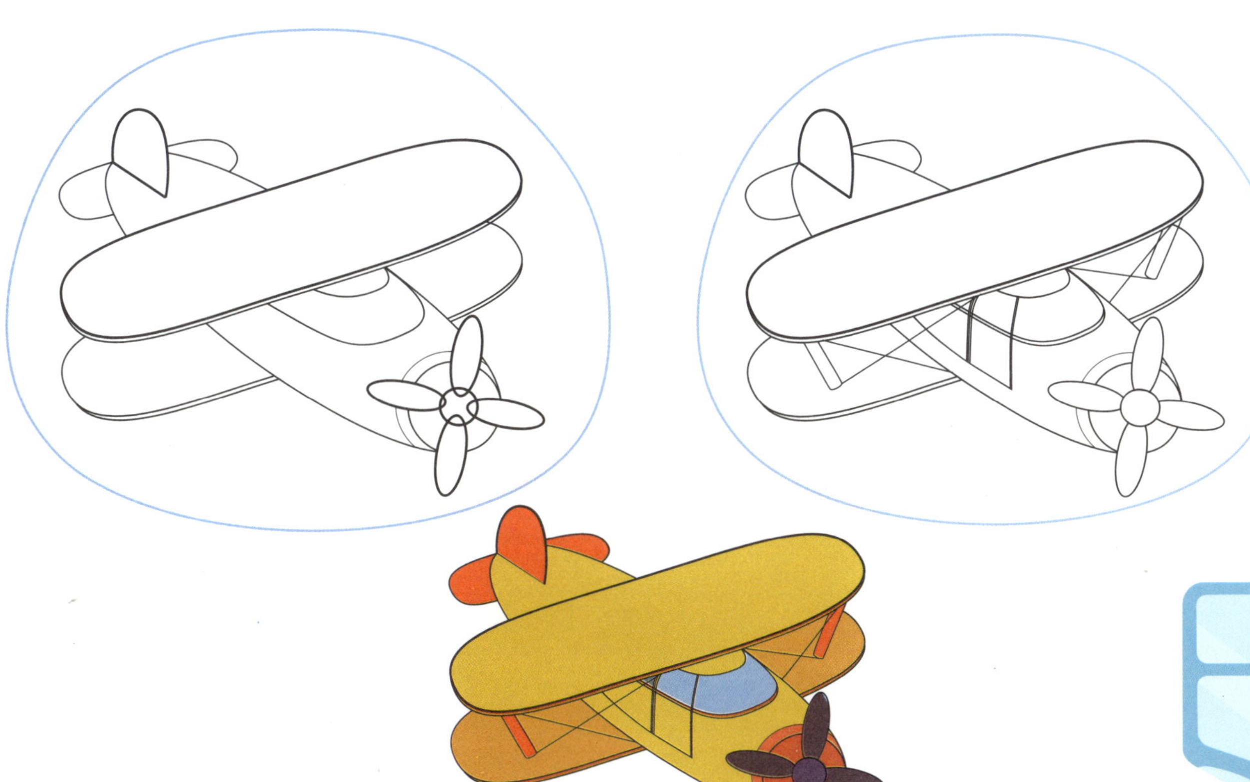

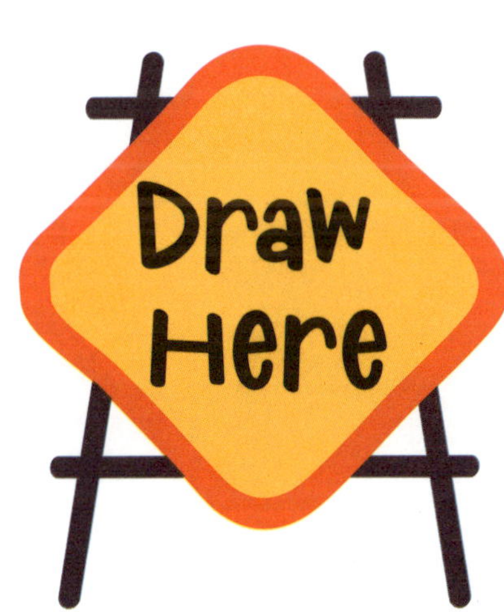

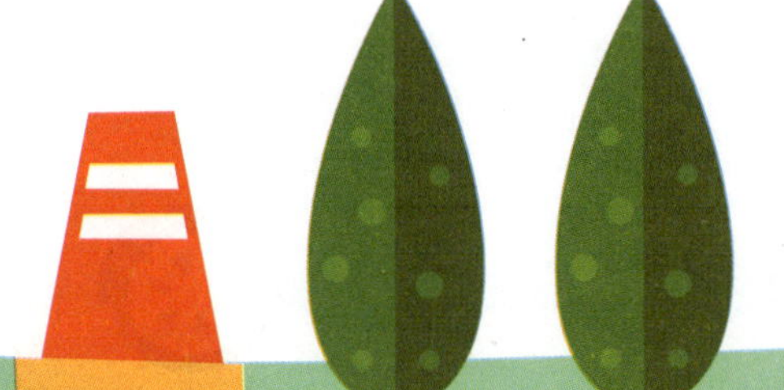

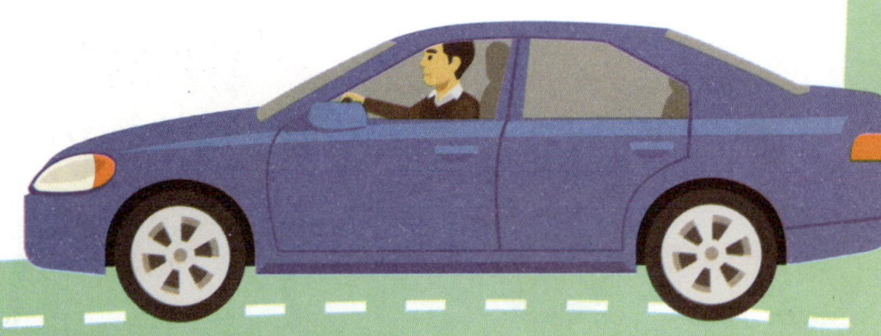

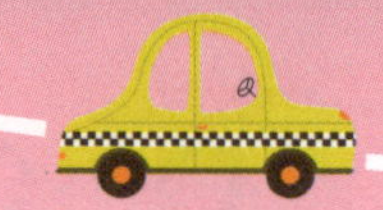

SCOOTER

This is a scooter. It's a light two-wheeled open motor vehicle.

1 Draw two tyres.

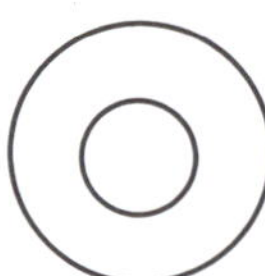
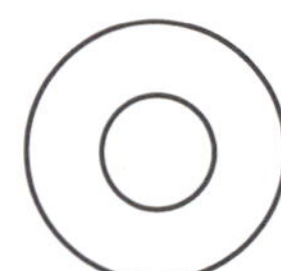

2 Draw a line connecting the back tyre with the body of the scooter.

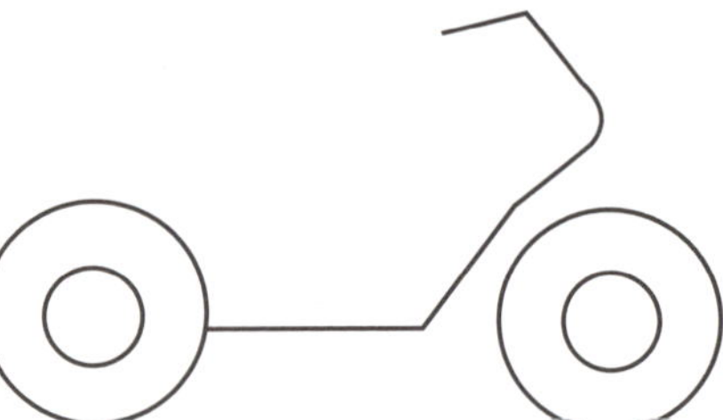

3 Draw the body of the scooter and its handles.

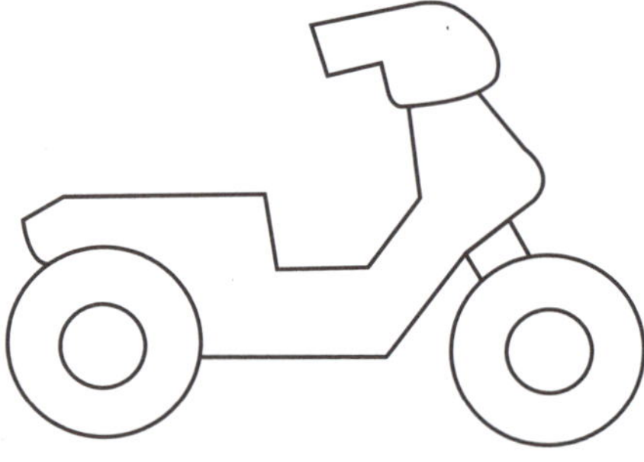

4 Draw its head light and brake light. Colour to complete.

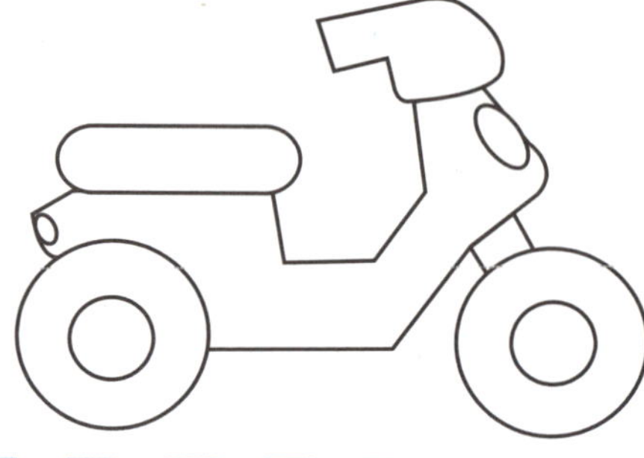

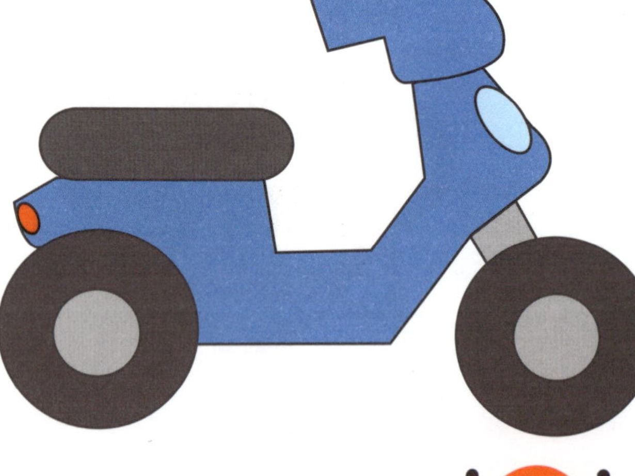

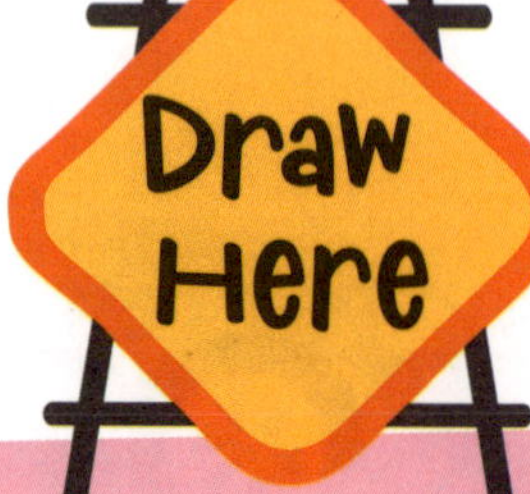